The WITCH'S GOSPEL

CHARLES BOWNESS

ROBERT HALE · LONDON

First published in Great Britain 1979

ISBN 0 7091 7619 8

Robert Hale Limited
Clerkenwell House
Clerkenwell Green
London EC1R 0HT

To
my Mother

Printed in Great Britain by
Clarke, Doble & Brendon Ltd,
Plymouth and London

CONTENTS

ACKNOWLEDGEMENTS

My thanks are due to the following persons for their help and encouragement: Max Riess for his patience and excellent photographs; the Scunthorpe *Evening Telegraph* for permission to reproduce the Haxey Hood photograph; to T. F. Cranidge for his invaluable advice; to other unselfish helpers such as Mrs D. Dent for information about the Isle of Axholme, and to Mrs B. Whitingham and Mrs S. Jacklin.

LIST OF ILLUSTRATIONS

All the photographs were taken by Max Riess with the exception of that of 'Smoking the Fool' which is reproduced by courtesy of the *Scunthorpe Evening Telegraph.*

I

THE ORIGINS OF THE FERTILITY CULT

Over many centuries witchcraft has evolved from a palaeolithic fertility cult into a loose set of beliefs with additions from Babylon, Chaldea, Egypt, Greece, Scandinavia, and many other areas. Besides these accretions there have been others which have been parodies of various contemporary religions. Despite all these additions, including such artificial ones as cabbalistic sorcery, the true derivation of witchcraft is the primitive fertility cult.

There are several ancient legends concerning the origins of witchcraft in which traditionally heavenly beings choose to mate with human women. One such story is the Babylonian one of Lilith and Shamash. A story of the coming down to earth of the sons of God is also recorded in Genesis and the story of Noah in the Bible.

The whole point of such legends is that having assumed human bodies, these beings had defied the authority of heaven and were unable to resume their former spiritual status. In turn these exiles fathered sons who were also of giant stature and possessed of unearthly wisdom. Magical knowledge was thus introduced into the world of human beings.

Some of the descendants of the fallen angels used their wisdom for good ends, but others resorted to every sort of evil. This unfortunately released wickedness into the world as well as wisdom. The evil spread and outweighed the good so that the original sons of God, appalled by what they had bred into the world, decided to destroy the worst areas of it in an attempt to compensate for their own original sin of lusting after the women of the earth.

The cataclysms which followed were on a global scale, of which we have geological evidence today. All peoples of the earth have legends about these great upheavals, volcanic eruptions, great floods and the like, and also race-memory stories about a time preceding them. These range from the 'dream-time' of the primitive people to the legends of the Manu of the Hindus, the Norse myths of a giants' revolt, the Greek parallels of the Titans, and the destruction of Atlantis, the biblical Garden of Eden, and the Flood.

There were however some survivors from the antediluvian culture who proved to be indestructible. They became spirits not of earth or of heaven, but the gods of witchcraft. Their powers are the sources of witchcraft power, and since their spiritual status is diminished to the extent that they are out of heavenly favour, they have to use human beings to activate their doings on earth. Among these alien spirits however, there are some who are able to reincarnate on earth and pass themselves off as human.

Witchcraft lies in a complex of fertility rites in which the reproductive forces of nature are personified. In one place the mother goddess is Venus, in others she is called Ashtoreth (or Astarte), Isis, Aphrodite, or Ishtar. Apart from regional considerations the names are unimportant for the mother goddess performs the same functions everywhere. A local variety of the common festival was the Letoia, called after the goddess Lete. She was worshipped under many names but was known as Lete at Hierapolis in Syria. A great festival celebrated the love of Lete for Adonis and Thammuz. This symbolized the yearly renewal and propagation of the animal and vegetable world.

Between the Tigris and the Euphrates lived a Sumero-Accadian people who practised magic in order to conjure up evil spirits. At the same time they prayed to beneficent gods.

The region was invaded by the Chaldeans and the old culture was superseded by worship of the sun-god known as Bel, Baal, or Marduk. The Chaldean priests were the first known practising astrologers, and were thereby able to combat the past influence of an elaborate system of demonology. They evolved a range of control methods which included divination, incantation, and conjuration. Besides the official priesthood there were scores of witches who used popular rituals that were considered to be extremely efficient.

The reason for their success was that they were in league with the demons to the extent of being able to assist them. These witches were noted for their proficiency with regard to imprecations, the use of effigies, and all the other familiar aspects of the Craft.

Influences of the Babylonian and Assyrian magical practices were felt throughout Asia Minor and biblical references from Genesis to Revelations reiterate the condemnation of false gods. The Jews often reverted to heathen practices and were just as often reprimanded and advised of the existence of one true God.

The magicians of Egypt were no less famous than their Chaldeo-Babylonian counterparts. Where the Chaldeans had worshipped Marduk, the Egyptian patron was Thoth who revealed the arts of music, geometry, writing and arithmetic, and also medicine and surgery. Under the authority of their divine headmaster the Egyptians were enabled to interpret dreams, cast nativities, and cure cases of spirit possession. No more than a drop of blood, some nail parings, or a piece of clothing incorporated into a modelled effigy was needed to make an irresistible charm. Higher initiates were credited with the ability to divide the waters. This accomplishment reflects that in the biblical record of the passage across the Red Sea.

One Egyptian witch-queen was Dalukah. She was feared because she made effigies of enemy armies, destroying them as it were by proxy. The last of the kings of ancient Egypt, Nectanebes, was credited with the same power. He also made small wax replicas of soldiers of the opposing armies and set them out on a large table. Over them he performed rites to promote victory to his own side. He would work out strategical movements which would later correspond in detail to the actual battles. 'War-gaming' is not unknown to several High Commands of today, often with a computer working in the role of predictor.

Isis was a witch-goddess and her name was much employed in formulae for the cure of diseases. That the Egyptians were inclined to witchcraft more than to sorcery is evidenced by their notable liking for love-charms, philtres, and spells.

Hebrew culture inherited the Babylonian varieties with all the fallen angels who were supernatural, but spiritual outcasts. These were again divided by the Jews into offspring of Eve by male spirits, and others descended from Adam by Lilith. It is held that Lilith represents the first completely Jewish witch. A charm used by Jewish women for protection against the powers of Lilith was to write upon walls Senoi, Sensenoi, and Semangelof, the names of three angels. Love-philtres were also popular among Jewish women. Aaron exercised his power over serpents before the Egyptians, and Daniel was a match for Nebuchadnezzar's magicians and astrologers.

Yet the Jews were only supposed to use magic in the name and service of God, in extreme circumstances. But they were prepared to use such power when Jehovah seemed too slow or severe for them. Saul banished those with familiar spirits, and wizards, yet when the occasion arose that he felt he could not gain assurance from Jehovah he soon consulted the witch of Endor.

There were however some minor exceptions to the laws proscribing witchcraft, for the Jews were allowed to interpret dreams, conduct some methods of prophecy, and their high priests used Urim and Thummim, two stones which they carried in a pocket of the ephod, a garment worn over the second tunic of their vestments. The stones were engraved respectively with an affirmative and a negative, and when one was taken out, the remaining stone represented the answer of the divine will.

Between 79 and 70 B.C. Simon ben Shetach caused eighty witches to be hanged, and when considered, it can be seen that Chaldean, Egyptian, and Jewish witches conformed closely to the type which became prominent in the Middle Ages.

A prominent part of ancient Mediterranean religious cults were the 'mysteries', such as those of Isis and Mithra. They were the means of satisfying the individual need for a dramatized faith with an assumption of immortality. But since they were often considered unofficial, being outside the recognized state cults, it was usually wise for initiates to be reticent about their activities.

Performance of rituals was a major part of the mystery cults and about 700 B.C. the Eleusinian mysteries conducted rites in which seeds were offered to Demeter the corn mother. The Greek word *mysterion* meant a rite performed in the presence of the initiated, but the meaning was eventually extended to mean a secret. The ancients desired personal spiritual experience, hoping for individual communion with the gods. Often they felt that the officially recognized religion could not satisfy their desires, and as a result the Eleusinian cult spread, as well as others connected with Orpheus and Dionysus.

Dionysus was incorporated into the Eleusinian tradition, which from about 600 B.C. also included the Orphic teachings. Apart from their legendary and allegorical character, the mysteries had the aim of raising the soul to divine status by providing the means of escape from the cycle of reincarnation. Their esoteric doctrines were designed to lead to higher wisdom for the initiates.

The same aims prompted the members of the Roman mysteries who inherited the Greek forms. But the Romans made several additions by adapting and introducing from oriental cults such as that of Cybele the great mother, who was really the Roman version of the fertility goddess long known in the ancient East under various names such as Isis, Ishtar, Rhea, and Astarte.

The Isis cults spread from ancient Egypt, but another great mystery came from ancient Persia. This was Mithraism, and Mithra or Mithras was regarded as the divine representative of the Supreme Being, Ahura Mazda. Roman armies spread the cult far and wide, for it was very popular among the soldiers, and several Mithraic shrines have been unearthed in Britain.

The belief that misfortune pursued those who neglected or angered the gods led to the placation of gods by the practice of making sacrificial gifts. Certain persons seemed to possess the ability of selecting the most efficient forms of sacrifice as well as the best ways of presenting them. Such persons became known as experts, those who were familiar with, and knowledgeable about, the ways and moods of the gods.

Repetition of formulas which were apparently successful resulted in regular set forms of words, prayers, and incantations, and recognized rituals. Naturally enough, the expert operators became the priests and priestesses. Through constant experiment and by the demands of the tribes, the priests learned how to placate the anger of the gods, and gradually the nature of rituals and sacrifices changed. The priests began to attempt to assume some of the powers of the gods, and so magic and sorcery were practised.

With this assumption of greater power more demands were made upon the priests. They were expected to ensure hunting success, victory in battle, and safety of the tribe. They were also expected to have the power to control winds, avert storms, cause necessary rainfall, and tame animals.

There were regional variations in the necessity for these powers, and often a division of power so that one man might be credited with a control over wild beasts, while another would become notable as a rain-maker.

When northern tribes reached Greece and Rome they brought versions of fertility worship from a different climate. Existing beliefs merged with those of the newcomers, Minoan and Etruscan culture mingled with northern ideas. With the borrowings from Egypt and Carthage the worship of Isis became recognized throughout the Roman Empire by about A.D. 69.

The witch of Christian times was a descendant of several branches of the cult. She had an inheritance from the Jewish witch and also from the witch families of Persia, Greece, and Rome. In the Greek pantheon of gods for example, there was a considerable place for the witch, and Hecate who was originally an ancient deity of Thrace gradually assumed the attributes of Cybele, Isis, and others. Hecate worship varied in different areas of Greece. Statues of Hecate were consulted as oracles. She was an arch-witch, often regarded as the personification of evil. A mistress of the arts of herbal lore, she was the mother of the witches Circe, Medea, and Scylla.

Syrian witches and those of Thessaly were also skilled in both beneficent and maleficent practices. They were experts in the use of narcotic ingredients such as aconite, belladonna, hyoscyamus, and opium, and the Syrians in particular were supposed to be shape-shifters, turning into wolves and hyenas at will. The Persians also had a thriving cult of witchcraft. All of this influenced the Greeks and in turn the Romans.

Like the pythoness of Greece, the sybil of Rome was a priestess as well as a witch. The main legend concerning witchcraft in Italy is that of Diana the moon goddess. Her brother Lucifer represented the sun. Following the usual tradition, an incestuous relationship of these two symbols produced a daughter. Her name was Aradia, or Herodias, and she became the patroness of the witches. How soon Diana herself came to be regarded as queen of the witches is doubtful.

The Italian '*strege*' or witches are the direct descendants of the Latin '*striges*' who got their name from the screech-owl, a night bird of ill-omen, and Diana sent her daughter Aradia to teach men and women the arts of witchcraft. The best witch in the Craft in each generation is granted twelve special powers from Aradia.

When Diana the moon fell in love with her brother Lucifer the light or sun, she accomplished her incestuous relationship by means of a magical trick. She assumed the form of a cat which slept on his bed, taking her own shape again in the darkness. Lucifer was furious after he discovered his unwitting sin, but by her power to give sleep Diana soothed his anger.

Though light and dark were united, they retained their own powers and aspects, but these powers were combined in their daughter Aradia. When Aradia was sent to earth by her mother, she taught people to adore the spirit of Diana at each full moon and to learn the secrets of her Craft. She also taught ways of freedom from moral and physical slavery. Her task accomplished, Aradia was recalled by her mother, but remains constantly available to confer powers upon those who follow her teachings and who are enabled to conjure up her spirit.

The main shrine to Diana in Italy was at Nemi near the ancient town of Aricia. One opinion is that this old shrine was instituted by Orestes who also took the image of Diana into Greece from Taurica Chersonesus, where his sister Iphigenia was a Dianic priestess. Amongst many people Diana was confused with Vesta, the goddess of the home. At Rome a fire was continually kept lighted in her temple by virgin priestesses who had dedicated themselves to the service of the goddess.

Another divinity shared the temple of Vesta. She was Egeria, a water spirit. This nymph was so grief-stricken when her husband Numa died that Diana turned her into a fountain, since when she has been the patroness of the waters, and women made sacrifices to Egeria to ensure easy childbirth.

2

DRUIDS AND BRYTHONS

Continuing the legend of the post-Flood era, the survivors of the cataclysms escaped to other lands, including Britain. There they mingled with the indigenous people who were called the Brythons or Prytani, and who grew corn and kept cattle. Living in round encampments, they used bronze knives and swords and flint-tipped arrows as weapons.

Their religion was a nature worship and much concerned with the moon and stars, and was conducted inside circles of stone which were usually enclosed by a large bank of earth and a ditch, a kind of original witches' circle.

Early tribal man was a community member, an integral part of a group in everything he did, his mind being a component of a group mind. But over a long period of economic change a sense of individual personality developed. Obviously this process did not go on at the same pace everywhere. Even today there are remote areas without regular contact with larger settlements, owing to geographical separation by forests, swamps, or the mountains, deserts, or seas.

When the Druids made contact with the Brythons the fusion produced an increase in wisdom and knowledge. Children born of Celtic mothers and Brythonic fathers often displayed extraordinary psychic powers. The legendary Merlin was such a one.

The ordinary people were completely under the control of the Druids, who apart from their tutorial and religious functions held the judicial authority and legal administration, adjudicating in disputes over matters like inheritance, boundaries, and so on. They issued penalties and were responsible for their execution, and also had the powers of banishment and excommunication. Transgression against the religious laws of natural healing was severely punished. In contrast to this apparently beneficent activity were the snake pits into which human beings were flung, sometimes for purposes of divination.

It is generally accepted however, that in most respects the Druids were dispensers of profound wisdom, with elevated philosophical principles and high ethical ideals, representing what was best in ancient British life and culture. There is little doubt that Druidism made a great contribution to the early phases of British civilization, a civilization to be developed by Romans, Saxons, Danes, and Normans, to result in the Englishman and his cultural heritage.

Although the influence of Druidism is apparent in witchcraft, the real progenitor of the witch cult that made its appearance much later was of Teutonic origin, its practitioners being called '*wiccan*', a word akin to wit which in the original Anglo-Saxon meant 'to know', or 'to perceive'.

The Celtic tribes who peopled Europe thought it worthwhile to propitiate the gods. The 1st May was one of the important celebrations. It involved a ceremony to Beltane in which a special cake was baked and fires were kindled on the hills. The cake was ritually broken into fragments which were dedicated to birds and beasts of prey so that they would spare the flocks and herds.

The record of magic in Britain begins with the Druids although it had been a feature in the lives of people before the dawn of history. Druids were the priests of a pantheistic philosophy and their influence spread throughout the Celtic tribes of western Europe.

Julius Caesar wrote of them in his *Commentaries*. He discovered that their headquarters were in Britain. Men were regularly sent over from mainland Europe to be instructed and initiated into their rites and learning. They formed a link between prehistoric and medieval magic, having a vast knowledge of herbal lore for both magical and curative purposes.

It was from Britain that the order spread into Gaul and Germania and when the sons of noblemen were sent as novices for instruction and eventual induction into the priesthood, they were given a general and cultural education. They were taught mathematics, astronomy, elements of religious faith and sacred rites, natural philosophy, and bardic poetry.

The traditions were committed to memory instead of being written down, for the Druids were the guardians and exponents of an esoteric nature religion. Gods worshipped by these Celtic Britons were Taranis, a thunder god, Belinus who was a sun god, Belatucador was the war god, while Belisama was a goddess who represented the liberal arts and wisdom, while Lud was a sea god. There were other male and female deities of various aspects of nature, but special reverence was given to the sun, water, forest groves and high places.

Mistletoe berries, symbolic of life, were cut before augury from the oak trees by a white-robed priest, using a ceremonial golden knife which was slightly curved, like a small sickle. Associations with this rite survive in modern Christmas celebrations.

In each settlement a piece of land was deliberately left uncultivated, being given over to the malignant powers. This is sometimes thought to be the origin of certain bits of common land and of village greens.

It has been suggested but not proved, that the name Druid is a derivative of the Greek '*dryad*', which meant a nymph who presided over the woods. There may well be some connection since the Greek for oak was '*dry*', and Druid is often supposed to be from '*drus*', another form for oak. Certainly the Druids annually offered a sacrifice to Artemis, who was the Greek equivalent of Diana, and who incorporated the same virtues as the goddess of the woodlands and was a personification of the life of nature both animal and vegetable, as well as of rivers and streams. Artemis was also represented by the moon and the annual sacrifice to her was a form of repayment for the animals killed during the year. Oak leaves were used in all Druidic rites, the oak tree and mistletoe being sacred.

When the Romans invaded Britain many of the Brythons were forced to retreat northwards. Some reached the remote areas of Scotland and they became known to the Romans as Picts. This name is from the Latin '*pictus*' meaning 'painted'. The appellation was given because the Picts were well known for their adornments and for their script which they shared with the Brythons. They also painted pictures and for special occasions they coloured their bodies blue with woad.

There are certain witches today who are marked with a blue spot, and the well known expression true-blue means a lasting, fast colour, as well as describing a person who adheres rigidly to a sect or a principle.

The written language of the Picts was called ogham and their main area of influence originally spread from what is now Dundee to Inverness, and later extended to the Shetlands. They worked in silver and carved in stone, and possessed a unique art style. To cure certain illnesses they used charm-stones, round stones painted with circles in a brown dye.

So centuries before the Christian era began, the Druids of Britain were famous in Europe for their magic, their gifts of prophecy, and their healing skills. The written system of ogham was named after Ogmios, the Celtic god of learning. The degrees of their hierarchy were three, the Ovates, the Bards, and the Druids, all equal in status but different in function. The Ovates were the guardians of the sacred rituals and practised divination, while the Bards were poets and warriors, whereas the Druids formed a pontifical college which taught the secret knowledge, sat in judgement, and had the power to issue important declarations such as those of war or peace. All three degrees were often simply called Druids.

The chosen chief was elected for life and was known as the Arch-Druid, being virtual ruler of the Gallic people. To gain clairvoyant knowledge of a person or object, the Druid would place his magical staff upon the object and sing or chant spontaneously composed verses. The magical staff was made of rowan wood usually, but yew and hawthorn were also used. Bone divination was practised using the right shoulder blade of an animal, boiled clean of flesh. The future was read too from tree roots, the shapes of clouds, and the flights of birds.

Undoubtedly the most famous of the Celtic queens was Boadicea, the leader of the Iceni tribe. She led the Brythons against the Roman invaders and defeated them at Colchester. Boadicea was an Ovate and therefore a priestess. Such women were the daughters of Druids and were initiated in their youth and crowned with verbena as the insignia of their rank.

Another wave of Celtic people were the Tuatha de Danann who swept into Ireland, to be themselves superseded by the Miled or Milesians from Spain. The Tuatha de Danann are interesting as the ex-inhabitants of four oceanic islands, the remains of Atlantis. Southernmost of the islands was Finias, ruled over by Nuda who is identified with the ancient British king Lud after whom Ludgate in London is named. To the east lay Gorias, in the charge of Lugh, grandson of Danu after whom the Tuatha de Danann were named. Lugh is identical with the Welsh Llew. Murias, the western island, was ruled by Dagda, and the northernmost island of Falias was associated with the famous stone of destiny.

The stone is thought to be that referred to in Genesis, xxviii, 18–22. In Ireland it was used in Cashel at the coronations of the kings of Munster, which was then a separate kingdom. Then in A.D. 502 the stone was taken to Scotland by Fergus. It rested in Scone and in the eighth century the town became the capital of Pictavia. Fergus and his successors were all crowned on the stone until in 1296 Edward I took it to Westminster and had a coronation chair made for it, to be henceforth used by monarchs of England to the present time.

When the Tuatha de Danann, the people of Danu the earth mother goddess, were driven out of Ireland by the people of Miled they went to live in the green hillocks around the Sea of Maiol, now known to us as the area of the Hebrides. The green mounds, still numerous today, have given archaeological evidence of different occupations. Some have contained pre-neolithic debris, while some have stone burial cists which were probably Bronze Age. Yet there were many of the mounds which had houses inside them, and these houses were all of one period. Their inhabitants were of the Iron Age and the houses were lived in when the Romans ruled south Britain.

The archaeological evidence points to the houses having been built in the form of stone cells surrounding a portable tent of skins or of tanned leather. The passages between the stone cells were built small to take the weight of the stone roofs. Another branch of the Tuatha de Danann known as the Sith occupied Lewis and worshipped a sea god called Sithan aidh. He was the husband of Cailleach, a sort of Western Highland Diana.

There are many stories around Lewis and Skye of the visitations of blue men to later inhabitants of the islands. These blue men of the Minch were offered an annual libation of ale by people of Lewis up to recent times, to ensure bounty from sea and land in the forthcoming year.

As the sea gradually eroded the coastal plains the Tuatha and the Sith migrated to eastern parts of Scotland where they became a part of the main body of the warlike Pictish confederacy. To the people who colonized the islands at a later date, the Tuatha were a mysterious race of little folk who lived inside the hills. Since the newcomers themselves erected turf cabins in the open they soon invested the little people with qualities and powers not available to themselves. Houses of the type found in the Hebrides and elsewhere in Scotland have also been found in Cornwall and Wales and various parts of England. In the 1920s when archaeologists were working in East Anglia on excavations of Romano-British cemeteries they found skulls from which teeth had been extracted. It was then found that local people had often taken the teeth for use as charms against complaints such as rheumatism. Many skulls had a coin in their mouths with which to pay their fare to the 'other side'. Some skeletons had shoes on for their spirit journey, and food to sustain them. Lamps were also found in the graves to light the dead through their dark journey, and the skeletons of children had bells on their ankles to scare away evil spirits.

When Pythagoras took Eastern mysticism to the West, from Egypt to Greece, it is possible that he was unaware of the existence of the Druidical doctrine of metempsychosis in Britain at the time of his journeying.

The Celtic occupation of Britain has bequeathed to us many things, elements of language, art forms, fascinating legends. In my own part of the country, which is Lincolnshire, sheep are still sometimes counted in the Celtic fashion of Yan, Tan, Tethera,

Pethera, Sethera, and so on. It can be clearly seen from the foregoing how some of the stories of fairy folk arose.

It must now be shown how the various accretions of religious history, both pagan and Christian, have contributed to the cult of witchcraft.

3

ELVES AND FAIRIES

The term 'Teutonic' is a generic one which covers the Vikings, Norsemen, Norwegians, Danes, Swedes, Dutch, Germans and English, as distinct from Celtic, Latin, or Slavonic Europeans. In adopting some of the beliefs of the Mediterranean ancients, conquerors of the Roman Empire combined them with beliefs of their own which they had brought from the North where the existence of witches of a similar character were a feature of their chronicles and sagas.

The Galdrakinna of the Scalds has close resemblance to the Stryga, the female witch of Latin classicism. Freya had qualities in common with Vesta. Nixas or Nicksa, a sea god worshipped on the shores of the Baltic, of whom the 'Old Nick' of England is a descendant, shared attributes with Neptune.

Classic mythology coalesced with much of the mythology of the North, but in the northern idea of witches there was no feeling of irreligion. The possession of magical knowledge was considered desirable as it was an attribute of the great gods such as Odin himself. Some of the particulars of the northern doctrines correspond so exactly with those of the classics that it would seem that they must have a common ancestry. There was also a great deal of transference between the Teutonic and the Celtic tribes.

The alphabet of the early Northlanders was known as the futhorc, ideographs made up of vertical and angular lines known as runes from the Gothic *runa* meaning mystery or secret. The runes were held to have magical power and were used for spells as well as for recording historical events. Rune staffs were employed for prophecy and other purposes.

Runes came to be used as badges of rank, craftsmen's marks, and are even used by tramps and gypsies in Britain and hoboes in

America today, and also—possibly inadvertently—as cattle marks. Runes can be found on medieval buildings and old cathedrals and churches. They are scattered all over the areas penetrated by the Baltic peoples, and have been carried further since. The witches still use a runic alphabet.

By the eleventh century there had been successive invasions of Britain by Angles, Saxons, Jutes, Danes, and ultimately by the Normans. Inevitably the Druidic and Brythonic lore was overlaid by a mixture of beliefs, Roman, Celtic, Saxon, and Christian. The Saxons called the Brythons either elvenfolk or heathens, people of the heath.

But the Norsemen brought their own varieties of fairy folk such as the *duergar* or dwarfs. These *duergar* were diminutive natives of Lapland, Finland, and Latvia, who had themselves lived in caverns and forests and other hiding places to escape the Asiatic hordes which had from time to time swept across Europe.

The dwarfs were skilled in mining and the smelting of minerals, and possessed an uncanny knowledge of weather lore. Their Asiatic enemies had regarded them with awe, as holding title to supernatural powers. In the area of what is now North Germany they were known as *'kobold'*, from which word is derived the English goblin and the Scottish bogle.

In engaging in a guerrilla warfare against their persecutors, they harassed by stealth. This secretive warfare was most frustrating to the enemy who found it extremely difficult to combat, a situation with modern parallels.

In time it became considered good fortune to be spared from such mysterious harassment. This belief in good luck lingers on today in personal feeling and in collective occupations such as mining or seafaring.

Conquests in Britain by the Norsemen provided a regular traffic to these islands and the dwarfs were readily assimilated into the scene. Yet another name for the *duergar*, dwarves, or elves was the Scandinavian title of trolls, still used today. In Britain however they became fairies, gnomes, dwarves, elves, pixies, brownies, goblins, hobgoblins, boggarts, bogles, drows, knockers, bogeys, imps, dancers, kilmoulis, spriggans, and witch-men. Some of these names were later importations, such as 'fairy' from Norman France, and some were regionally adopted names.

Throughout the Norse mythology as well as in numerous fairy stories the elves played a prominent part. Sometimes they are depicted as troublesome, sometimes as helpful as in Tom Thumb, and Snow White. They are invariably known as a subterranean race inhabiting deep caves and places where horrible murders or other crimes had occurred, places shunned by the ordinary populace.

Tom Thumb probably represented a changeling, since the elves were sometimes supposed to carry off unchristened infants to rear as their own. Sometimes they would leave one of their own children as a substitute, though not always. Occasionally, the unwary adult was liable to be carried off if he exposed himself to the power of the elves. It was unwise to sleep in the vicinity of fairy hills and similar places. Some article or object would be found left behind, such as a shepherd's crook or a hat, as the only trace left of the missing person.

The reason for these kidnappings was usually due to the fact that the elves had to pay annual tribute to their gods of a human being. Substitution of a foreign person provided a satisfactory compromise.

There were occasional survivors who returned from 'fairyland'. They all appeared to agree that the splendour of life there had a curious propensity for turning into something else. The activities of the elfish courts, the lavish banquets, the costly jewellery and plate, the handsome men and richly-dressed beautiful ladies, all would suddenly and unaccountably turn into mean fare, the jewels and plate would become a shabby parody of stone and clay, while the handsome men and beautiful women would become ugly wrinkled old men and hag-like women in poor dress, and likewise when the glamour wore off the luxurious and stately courts would turn into dank, dismal caverns.

This theme of false banquets and the rest has often played a part in literature, as has the story of restoration to normal life such as in the one concerning Sleeping Beauty. The fairy tale, which was ancient legend, was given a literary form after 1630 by writers like Charles Perrault in France.

The ability to practise a certain type of hypnotic fascination known as the 'glamour' is much attributed to some members of the Romany race. The witches of the Germanic and Scandinavian tribes could make people believe that someone for whom they were searching was not actually present. The degree of Haxa was conferred upon the chief priests and priestesses, and the word 'hexe' or 'hex' is derived from this and came to mean either a witch or a witch's spell.

These elves shared similar attributes of the Celtic tribes in their love of valleys, rocks, and forests. Although notably capricious the elves did not totally shun the society of men, and though they were dangerous as enemies, could also be valuable as friends. They recognized the powers of witch deities whose spells could alter the course of the elements, changing the influence of the sun and thus causing its beneficial operation to be withdrawn from the crops and fruits, who could call down the power of the moon and disturb the course of nature.

The British fairy folk sometimes had a king, though much more often a queen was acknowledged. One such head of the order was Nicneven, who was the equivalent of the triple-named Diana, Hecate, or Herodias, the witch-goddess of Italy. Nicneven was notorious for her malignant power to raise terrible storms and other violent disturbances.

Merlin Wild or Wylt was the son of an elf who faithfully served the legendary champion of Celtic Britain, King Arthur. Merlin is perhaps the best known of the Druid wizards. A Welsh bard, he is associated with the cycle of the Arthurian romances. To give but one example of his prophecies, he foretold the way in which Earl Godwin would die. Earl Godwin was the father of the future king, Harold II. The Earl was dining with King Edward the Confessor, who was his son-in-law, when Edward made the remark that his brother Alfred would still be alive were it not for the Earl. Godwin protested his innocence, saying, "May this bread choke me if I am guilty". It was at that moment that he actually did choke to death. The island on which he had his house disappeared under the sea, to become that curse of mariners, the treacherous quicksands off the Kent coast known as the Goodwin Sands.

As the leader of an oppressed minority, King Arthur possessed all the attributes of the fairy-witch-kings, a coven of the round table, a magical sword, and a ritual priest in Merlin. Examples of such legendary figures abound throughout Europe.

Our ancestors thought of elves as potentially dangerous, having possibly malicious intentions, and therefore having to be placated, for although not the same as nature spirits, they were allied to them. A race apart, they had their own laws and rulers, their own occupations, and though living side by side with ordinary men had greater powers, to help, to injure, or beguile.

Men could and did visit the fairy lands, which were usually under the earth. There were even marriages between humans and the little folk. The elves were generally held to be rather on the wrong side of good, too bad for heaven, but too good for hell. They were universally feared and only witches could normally associate with them without incurring grave danger. It was risky for a human to partake of food or drink in fairyland, for the chances were they would never return to human society. The elves or fairies haunted barrows and other prehistoric burial places, but they were not tied to one spot but would move on elsewhere if they so desired.

Although their lives were in some respects similar to those of humans, they appeared and disappeared suddenly, stole children and left changelings, had organized tribal states, and they owned cattle and other domesticated animals. Living in houses entered through the sides of hills or through holes in the ground, the elves disliked being watched, and captured spies were severely punished.

Their favourite weapon was the elf-bolt or elf-shot, short arrows with stone heads. This was consistent with the memory of a Neolithic ancestry of people who were small, dark, and no more than four or five feet tall and who also lived in round huts with sunken floors well below ground level, and covered with turf to look like green mounds.

The origin of the 'craft of the wise' is therefore to be found in prehistoric religion. Nature was worshipped by primitive peoples in every area of the world. To recognize the background of Nature as one's environment was only logical, but the man or woman who was intelligent and imaginative enough to utilize Nature either for personal or community purposes was a person of individuality and outstanding character.

Such an individual would appear to have some command over his environment, however slight. He might be a fire maker, a leader, someone knowledgeable in herbal or weather lore, or a maker of weapons and tools.

Initially of course, the man who demonstrated his skill over Nature was the provider of food, the hunter. In pitting his wits and agility against the beasts of the plain and the animals of the forest, he was essential to the existence of the tribe. His mastery depended upon his ability to track down game and his cunning in being able to kill or capture it.

The hero was the skilled hunter who understood his environment sufficiently to enable him to survive confidently against the odds of Nature. His means of doing so often involved the arts of camouflage and decoy. Clad in the skin of an animal, with horns or antlers, he would get close enough to the herd to stampede it into some prepared trap.

It might be offered as a theory that women discovered or invented agriculture. Since they remained behind when the hunters were out on an expedition, it may be conjectured that they observed the growth of cast away seeds.

However this may have been, in the course of time many people settled down to become cultivators, and new arts were required. Each change meant an extension of vocabulary and the means of spoken communication developed and evolved and knowledge could be retained in the mind. Instead of simple instinct alone, the way of reasoning faculty opened more and more. Nature was the fertile goddess of creation and with knowledge of her ways, men could use her powers.

The hunter gave way to the husband, in the original sense of the word, the husbandman, the dweller, the householder and tiller of the soil. Having captured some of the resources of Nature man was entitled to feel some sense of mastery as well as kinship with the goddess with whom he worked as well as tried to subdue to his needs. Yet he could never account for all her fickle ways or ever completely conquer her, and so with the respect that is born of fear, he worshipped her.

Nature had pitfalls for the unwise and the unwary, but also blessings for those who shared some of her secrets and showed devotion.

And so emerged two great main deities, representing the male and female aspects. The first god of the man was the horned hunter who was the spirit of masculine virility, and then came the nature goddess, the womb of all creation. Both of these aspects alternated between a harmonious relationship and an uneasy one.

Thus was the origin of the craft of the wise.

ıree Books of Shadows, in ıich the witch records ells, rites, herbal recipes ıd a history of the Craft.

he jewellery of witches cludes copper and silver racelets and necklaces of eads in multiples of nine thirteen.

Keys, a glass float and a fairing, or glass 'walking stick', to keep evil spirits away from the home.

A bolline, a type of atha[illegible] with a curved blade.

4

THE COMING OF THE NEW FAITH

In direct contrast to the elves and fairies phenomenon were the giants such as the legendary Titans of the Greeks. They were the children of the sky father Ouranes and the earth mother Gaia, being another version of the 'sons of God' story.

Long, long ago, our own island was supposed to have been inhabited by giants who were brutal, stupid, and given to cannibalism. It is said that when Brutus the Trojan landed from Gaul he met these giants who hurled boulders when angry. It has also been suggested that they built menhirs and circles of stones such as Stonehenge, but there is no evidence to support this.

When Troy fell to the Greeks, Brutus and some of his Trojans are believed to have fled and eventually to have arrived in Britain where he was opposed by a band of giants which he defeated.

The giants were led by Gog and Magog. This is confusing since these names are mentioned in Genesis also. However, after defeating the giants the Trojans moved on to London where, at the junction of the Fleet and the Thames, they built a town which they called New Troy. Brutus's palace was erected on the spot which later became the site of the Guildhall.

Medieval chronicles tell of two giants called Gog and Magog who acted as palace porters. For many years huge wickerwork figures of the pair featured in mayoral processions. The Gogmagog Hills are near Cambridge.

The famous representation of a giant cut in the Sussex chalk hills and known as the Long Man of Wilmington, is 240 feet high. There is a Cerne Abbas Giant, and there is the old legend of Goram and Vincent who were each over 40 feet in height and who shared one enormous pickaxe while cutting a channel for the River Avon through the rocks. One day Goram fell asleep while his brother was working, and consequently did not hear him shout as he hurled the pickaxe from 3 miles away at the end of his stint. It struck Goram on the head and he died from the blow. Lonely and heartbroken, Vincent buried his brother in the sea and piled up huge rocks from a glen called Coombe Dingle, making it so high that the sea could not cover it, thus forming Dunball Island.

Cormoran and his wife Cornelian built Saint Michael's Mount, and Bolster was another Cornish giant along with Corcoran and Blunderbore. Manchester had a giant called Tarquin who lived at Knot Mill and who was slain by Sir Lancelot, and near Hartlepool the monster Grendel held sway until he was killed by Beowulf who has a mythical association with the area. The original 'Jack' of giant-killing fame came from Land's End and became tutor to King Arthur's only son.

Perhaps the best-known giant to the layman is the biblical Goliath, also destroyed by courage and superior skill. All of the giants, unlike the fairy-folk, were eventually killed off. But to the magical tribes of the elves, with their witch counterparts, a new and more subtle threat was about to challenge their existence.

The Roman Christianization in Britain had no deep or lasting effect after the power of the Roman Empire crumbled away. It was felt to be in part a political conversion to obedience to Roman rule, an importation from outside which was naturally resented. By A.D. 455 the power of the old Roman Empire had declined and what was emerging was the Holy Roman Empire, basing its claims on spiritual authority. Although Saint Augustine landed from Rome in A.D. 597, his area of influence was mainly in Kent where he had converted King Ethelbert who ruled that area, and although Augustine was declared Archbishop of England in 601, the title was not as comprehensive as it suggests.

The conversion to Christianity was a slow and piecemeal affair, largely dependent on the conversion of kings and others of influence. Although ultimately Britain became nominally Christian, for a long time the new faith had to exist alongside the old religion of witchcraft, and even the kings were dualistic in their approach to the matter.

Difficulty in enforcing Christianity upon the populace is evidenced by the many decrees issued. For example the Emperor Justinian who died in A.D. 565 devoted a part of his famous codification of Roman law to dealing with witchcraft, and 250 years later Charlemagne enacted even stricter laws for its suppression.

In the seventh century Bishop Barbatus had a certain tree in his diocese cut down because witches met by it. King Ethelred banished witches, soothsayers, and magicians, as did Canute the Danish king who also claimed the English throne, and who married Ethelred's widow.

Yet in its early days at least, as an organization Christianity was compelled in practice if not in admitted theory, to come to terms with the strength of the old pagan customs it was trying to supersede. Many of the popular customs and pagan festivals were adapted into Christian observance and pagan deities were 'baptized' and often canonized, as in the case of Saint Walpurg. Many springs and wells were associated with her. Oil was said to exude from her bones on Walpurgis Night, and this oil could relieve certain pains such as toothache and the pains of confinement. Walpurg had a long history as a witch-goddess, and was also credited with the cure of hydrophobia.

In a similar manner the worship of the mother-goddess Diana runs parallel with that of the Virgin Mary. At the same time the early Christian fathers tried to curtail the pagan element by denunciation and by forbidding singing and dancing on saints' days.

Another measure taken to combat witchcraft was that of declaring that since Christianity was a monotheistic religion there could be no rival god and so the horned god of the pagans could not be assimilated into the religion except in the role of an enemy, and so by a process of constant denunciation, the horned god became identified with the Devil.

In adapting for their own uses certain pagan rites and beliefs the Christians were only following the example of predecessors. When he had denounced political and religious enemies who were undermining his theocratic state, the ancient Jewish king was doing what popes did later on in their anathemas against backsliding Christians.

Then as now there was a literate class proclaiming its own

orthodoxy. Any other practices were regarded as dangerous folly. Witchcraft at the mass level was reviled as being a menace to the establishment of Christianity, a challenge by the unprofessional.

In making known their astrological forecasts concerning a new King of the Jews, the Persian Magi challenged the supremacy of King Herod, and invited his wrath. Witchcraft had long been regarded as politically suspect and spiritually dangerous.

Emperors, kings, and statesmen had a natural dislike of prophets who predicted their overthrow or misfortune. Another fear was that such prophecies encouraged people to ensure that they came to pass by means of assassination. Witches had always held a great knowledge of herbs and there were always political enemies willing to recruit such knowledge for their own ends. This partly explains why the later history of witchcraft has been one of denigration from the established professional classes.

In the eighth century Pope Gregory issued instructions saying that deep-rooted pagan customs which were hard to eradicate should be turned into Christian ones. Through this process many pagan gods and goddesses became Christian saints. One of them was Lugh whose name is the Celtic form of Lucifer or Lux, the light or the sun. By a strange twist of belief, Lugh was turned into Saint Michael. Yet it was supposed to have been Michael who had expelled Lucifer from heaven.

Despite sporadic persecution peasants in the fifth century had carried effigies in procession, pitiful representations of the old gods. Such pagan processions were still being noted in the eighth century, and were still happening 400 years later.

In 1389 these activities were again condemned and deplored by the authorities. Prohibition was still being suggested in 1400, and astrology in particular was singled out as a persistent threat to authority.

With a thoroughness born of conscious virtue, the new order of Christianity attempted to stamp out paganism. But because of excessive zeal on the part of the official religion, the old one survived partly in secret.

It became supposed by the Christians that such persistent heresy could only be the work of the Devil. The cleverest of them tried to utilize the heresy itself by pressing into service the pagan gods, converting them into useful saints and using some of their festivals as saints' days.

Any pagan activity left over from such proselytizing activity could then be regarded as wilful heresy or magical in origin. As the Church gained more and more of the civil power, the pagan was increasingly attacked without mercy. It was intolerable to the Church to allow opposition from people who were believed to have communication with supernatural powers. But the result of all this denunciation was to strengthen belief in the power of the witch. It appeared that what constituted such a threat must have a very real existence.

At the same time the existence of witchcraft provided the later Church with a more or less permanent enemy which could be held up as an example of a challenge to right-thinking orthodoxy. The wicked infidel abroad could also be used as an example of heresy, but an enemy in the midst of the people at home could be utilized regularly with wider effect. Public suppression of witches could demonstrate the power of the Church practically.

All of these attentions from the Church resulted in a lot of reported tradition and precedent growing up about the witch cult. By the eleventh century both Church and people were able to draw upon this collection of information and were at liberty to add embellishments.

When the Church establishment found that it had failed to dislodge Old Nick from Britain and it was felt to be expedient to canonize him as promptly as possible and thus appropriate him to her own use, she knew that any other move at that time would have angered the populace.

It was much later that Old Nick was declared to be the Devil, and this was to those people who still used his name for their horned god. Many places having pagan legends are near to or are connected with churches, abbeys, or saints' names, because early Christians built their churches in places already considered as sacred. This was deliberately done with the idea of attracting followers of the old religion to the new faith.

But in those early days both religions often worked alongside each other without any animosity, even to the extent that at least one church contained two altars, one for pagan worship, the other for Christian.

It was when the established Church realized that the old faith presented too powerful a rival that they began changing the old gods into demons, or alternatively canonizing them and declaring all non-Christians to be heretics who must be persecuted as such.

This process occurred all over the Christian world. Witch wells and other pagan spots in England acquired holy status and the healing properties attached to them came within the province of the Church. Or so it was thought. Mediterranean grottoes once occupied by elementals such as nymphs and naiads were accredited to the new saints.

It was a long and difficult task to enforce orthodoxy in remote places like Britain. The earliest missionaries could only make conversions in limited localities. There were vast areas in which there was only a flimsy notion of what was happening. People also tended to relapse into paganism after some of the invasions by the Norsemen.

Then when a semblance of religious stability was finally achieved, it was only because most people adopted Christianity as a political necessity. Saint Olaf was one who tried to exterminate paganism with such severity, that to those under his domination in Norway it was a choice between baptism or death.

Many poor people accepted baptism only for the sake of the ritual robes, which were presented to them as a gift. In this they were rather like the 'rice-Christians' of a much later date in the Far East.

Belief in witchcraft was the prime target of the zealots who regarded pre-Christian survivals as an insult to the new faith.

5

THE RESURGENCE OF WITCHCRAFT

On the credit side it must be said that Christianity offered a form of worship to all classes, and since it was monotheistic it could give simple concentration, and much of its symbolism was easy to comprehend. The emphasis was upon redemption for the individual and yet there was allowance for community sense in many of the ritual observances providing for emotional release. Incidentally the communion of the Agape or 'love-feast' held in early times required a group of thirteen people. Another aspect of Christianity which tended to ensure its popularity was that women were supposed to be allowed into the faith as equals.

Despite the attempts to suppress pagan worship, it should not be supposed that the new religion engendered no enthusiasm. A Christian fervour eventually spread through Europe, enabling the establishment of convents and monasteries to take place. When all this had happened it was supposed that pagan worship had finally been supplanted.

Christianity also held the appeal of parallels, an appeal which the Church was not slow to recognize. It had similarities with Mithraism, particularly in relation to the Holy Communion and the 'eating of the god'. Eastern peoples in the Egyptian tradition could recognize in the Holy Trinity a substitution for the old triad of Osiris, Isis, and Horus.

The idea of a mother goddess did not seem to be lost when the Virgin Mary became regarded as the main intermediary between humans and the Almighty.

Yggdrasil was a mystical ash tree which in Norse mythology typified existence. It bound together earth, heaven, and hell by means of its roots and branches, thus forming another trinity. There was also the tree of knowledge of good and evil in the Old

Testament. Northern people could readily recognize their familiar symbol of Yggdrasil in the Cross, and so transfer their tree worship into Christian terms, for the Cross also had three points.

Many such parallels could be argued, and although the later Church utilized some of them, it is only fair to say that in the early days at least it did not do so, and the transferences were made by the people themselves, many of whom must have thought they were hearing in the Christian doctrine a newer version of the old traditions with which they were so familiar.

In setting up its campaign of conversion the early Church had a great deal to combat. It had to offset Mediterranean ritual, and Druidism, and to contend with Scandinavian and Teutonic magic. In the remote scattered villages of Britain only the sketchiest knowledge of Christian doctrine was held by the illiterate poor, and dialects were spoken that were largely incomprehensible to those at court and in the Latinist monasteries.

Small wonder then that misunderstanding and unconscious parody occurred.

Gradually however the Church established a wider spiritual unity and the nation became recognizably cohesive as racial differences became blurred. The old beliefs became the tenets of an even smaller minority. The cult of witchcraft became surreptitious and clandestine, its members having to pay at least lip service to Christianity.

Yet this minority throughout the land never forgot its old shrines and the old associations. Witchcraft survived amongst those who recalled the ancient palaeolithic fertility practices and remembered the Norse mythology, and when from time to time the severities of the ascetic Church became too much for the poor of feudal times, witchcraft gained new adherents to its covens.

The Holy Office, better known as the Inquisition, was the inquiry instituted by Pope Innocent IV in 1248. Its purpose was the official organized suppression of heresy. Any suspect could be brought before the tribunals on the most fragile evidence. Even allowing for exaggeration, the Inquisition and its ramifications were responsible for thousands of deaths and a vast amount of suffering.

In the fourteenth century, 300 years later, the Church was still trying to stamp out 'heresy' and more than a mere nominal conversion was required. Where previously many of the old beliefs and customs had been overlooked, and compromise allowed to the extent of attaching saints' names to places hallowed by tradition and so forth, it was now clear that the Church demanded that her supremacy must be acknowledged by all.

The time for compromise was over with the establishment of the Inquisition. A horrified Church discovered that the fertility cult worship was still a major form of religion. The influence of Nordic culture still held sway from the East Anglian fens to the moors of Yorkshire and the wilds of Scotland. In Wales and Cornwall the Celtic language and heritage had never been forgotten and in many instances was supreme.

Although initially Christianity had held some appeal for women, when it was well established many began to feel that the position of women in the Church was a relatively low one. The Virgin Mary held a spiritually privileged role, but her attributes were not reckoned to pertain to the generality of females.

A few women could attain to the rank of abbess, but even as heads of convents were debarred from the priesthood, unlike their male counterparts. Certainly some abbesses in England and Germany were very powerful, but even so it was a position limited to the few.

Outside holy orders the aristocratic lady of the Middle Ages had to content herself with the somewhat static role of being an object of chivalry, whilst her poorer sisters were seen as little more than a potential source of evil temptation.

The strictures of such an ascetically inclined Church caused many to examine their position. From their ivory towers or their wattle huts there were only two avenues of escape for women who resented subjugation, either to the deprivations of the nunnery or the apparent if secretive liberty of the witch coven.

Punishments given out by some of the Church authorities for non-observance were so severe that they drove many people to revolt and the Inquisition claimed that a wave of witchcraft spread across Europe. Despite the arbitrary nature of Inquisition investigations and trials, the truth of the claim is not an improbable one.

The initiation of children into the old religion of their parents was with some a natural family custom. These hereditary witches and the socially frustrated women were only some of the recruits to the witch cult. Others were drawn from people who were afraid or ashamed of Christian confession, or who were merely rebellious against what they saw as imposition. There were also many who felt they could obtain advice or relief which they could not get from the Church.

To women the cult had always been popular. Firstly the Dianic and Aradian mother-goddess aspects had appeal, and secondly there was the offer of equality that was so much less evident within the confines of the Church. The ancient fertility rites of worship had always recognized women as the producers of life and mistresses of the hearth and home. Matriarchy had been common to some older social systems, as it still is with many gypsy tribes of today. Women were the main custodians of kitchen herbal lore, and were in an advantageous position to pass on their knowledge to the children.

In witchcraft this special role was always acknowledged, but within the Craft there was always equal opportunity for both sexes, because the necessity of both was recognized in the rituals.

Again in 1484 the Church realized that the witch cult was persistent and perpetuating and Pope Innocent VIII declared formal war on the heresy of witchcraft. Two years later the *Malleus Maleficarum* was published. It became known as the official book for the finding of witches and the conducting of witch trials. This book was soon popularly known as the 'Hammer of the Witches', and was extensively used by both Catholic and Protestant witch hunters.

The hopeful supposition that the changes of history and the activities of the Church had resulted in the dwindling of the old forms into mere folklore legend was now officially shown to be a false one.

Witchcraft is in large part concerned with the unseen and where this touches the psyche of mankind. When the influence of

Christianity spread across Europe, many who belonged to the old religion or wished to join it were moved to reaffirm or affirm their allegiance. The performance of a symbolic repudiation has given rise to the popular story of the Lord's Prayer being recited backwards, regarded by many as being the epitome of sacrilege. This particular recital has been seized upon avidly by many writers as an example of the horrible practices of witchcraft. It has been grafted on to many fictitious stories of black magic and has consequently been seriously accepted as a ritual by sensation seekers.

In fact the repudiation of Christianity took different forms in different places and the reversed Lord's Prayer was only one such form. It was usually felt that whatever had sufficient psychological impact on the member of the coven was enough to cause him to cast off the shackles of the new order by offering at least a token resistance. It then gave the member the feeling of freedom of choice in the face of what was held to be a spiritual and political coercion.

Some covens performed a blood pact, and it may be imagined how deeply shocked and offended the powerful Church authorities were at such practices of defiance.

Unfortunately the practice of Christianity had itself suffered some degeneration over the years since its foundation. As the legitimacy of the faith became acknowledged and its earliest adherents were able to emerge from their catacombs and their groups of thirteen amongst the pagans and their other refuges, the break up of the secret cells ensued and the way was then open for all sorts of pathological misfits to flock to the new Church. Some of these spiritual escapists promoted their own peculiar brands of ascetic masochism. Literally thousands of people became fakirs practising various forms of hysterical fervour ranging from self-castration to pole-squatting and flagellation.

To some extent it seemed that the religion of love had become debased into the kind of fakir and dervish activity still endemic in the East today. Some of the practices such as flagellation lingered on well into the Middle Ages and even afterwards.

Not everybody wished to join a religion made notorious for self-torture and ascetic punishment, but the persecution of such people was to last through more than another two centuries.

6

THE CONTINUANCE OF WITCHCRAFT

The decline of overt witchcraft groups caused by pressure from Church and State resulted in many people becoming lonely practitioners of white, grey, or black aspects of the Craft. These people were compelled to become either isolated 'cunning men' or 'wise women', or alternatively where possible to share their knowledge with a few others of similar conviction within limited areas. And in spite of all the persecution, to thousands of the inhabitants of Britain it was a case of 'better the devil you know than the devil you don't'. Wise men and women were at least able to provide herbal cures for men and animals, a service useful to the poor in the absence of the advice of physicians, and in the activities of a coven could be found emotional release.

So the witch cult contrived to survive. Admittance by initiation was almost always sponsored by existing witches. Rites were subject to variation in different districts. In every case however there was a formal introduction to the coven followed by the initiate taking an oath in much the same way as anyone might in joining any society of serious intent. The much publicized 'pact with the Devil' was in reality a confirmatory vow of loyalty made to the coven leader before the rest of the group.

Some covens required a signature or mark made in blood appended to some form of covenant, but most covens did not. This idea of a written contract was a much later addition to witchcraft and since many could neither read nor write it had a limited value. It was also a dangerous practice as in the wrong hands it could provide evidence against the witches. Its real purpose was to impress the novice with the solemnity of the occasion, and of how irrevocable was its nature.

The point in these medieval ceremonies was an avowal of denial of the Church and declaration of allegiance to the witch cult, and this was the sin of heresy so detested by ecclesiastical authority. Practices of initiation varied as they were often a matter for local inventiveness. Sometimes they involved the kind of juvenile practical joking indulged in at apprenticeship revels or in public schools. In some cases there were degrees of unpleasantness right down to sheer obscenity. It all depended on the kind of coven and its membership.

New witches were given a secret name to be used only by other members. This is the common feature of societies of a secret kind with titles like Grand Master, Imperator, Chief Elk and so forth. It follows too the universal habit of 'nicknaming' from schoolboy sobriquets to family names of affection. Obviously security was all important and the promise of loyalty was a necessity.

The killing and rebirth of nature gods is an integral part of pagan worship. This is exemplified in many folk songs and dances in which a Wild Man or similar figure is killed and then brought back to life by the Doctor, Master, or Wizard. Mediterranean peoples represented the annual decay and revival of life under the names of Tammuz, Adonis, Osiris, and Attis.

The harvest always required a 'mother' who could be praised for her abundance of production. From this feeling arose the ceremonies dedicated to corn mothers and corn maidens which proliferate throughout Europe. This idea is still recognized by the Church today in the Harvest Festival. This antique idea has been in practice all over the world and was in favour with Stone Age lake dwellers. Demeter was the Greek goddess of corn and harvests generally, and was known to the Romans as Ceres, from which name we get the word 'cereal'.

The last sheaf cut in the field meant the annual death of the corn mother, and the conclusion of the harvest was joyfully celebrated. This last sheaf was the important symbol, and the continuance of procreation had to be ensured. In many places it was made up into the shape of a woman, the corn dolly. It was carried home borne aloft to become the centre piece of the harvest supper and dance.

With some it was customary to give the straw to the cattle afterwards, in the belief that the spirit of the corn mother would make them thrive throughout the year. The corn dolly or puppet made from the sheaf was dressed in clothing like a doll and hung up in the barn until a new one was made at the next harvest.

All of these fertility customs are similar in structure having a death and resurrection theme involving two major elements such as the sun and the moon. Or there was a divine birth from the division of a single parent. These twin divisions were invariably concerned with the story of one twin who is lost or stolen, and in which the other must search for it in order to re-establish unity in Nature.

Hundreds of stories in European mythology have been woven from this fundamental theme of the adventures of a seeker, and perhaps the best known Norse account of the tradition of understanding and defeating death is that of Freya's search for her brother Frey.

Greek mythology has the story of the search by Hermes for Persephone. He found this daughter of Demeter or Mother Nature in the underworld, a captive of Hades. Persephone was then allowed half of her time with her mother Ceres on earth, but had to spend the rest of her time in the underworld.

In natural terms this represents the division of summer and winter. Orpheus's search for Eurydice is another version, and so is that concerning Dionysus and Semele. The occult legends from different areas resemble each other in theme, but have variations according to locale. As we have previously seen, the Herodias or Aradia of the Italian witches is the mediatory spirit between them and her mother Diana the moon goddess, whose counterpart is Lucifer, the light on earth.

And to Nordic witchcraft the tree Yggdrasil was a sacred symbol of the relationship between heaven and earth or the higher and lower aspects of existence. This sort of symbolism occurs throughout occultism, other examples being seen in the Babylonian ziggurat or pyramid of seven planes, in the tree of life of the cabbalists, the system of chakras of yoga, and the ladder of primitive Shamanism. The ascending of such spiritual obstacles gives to the seeker a series of degrees of achievement or mental awakenings.

The legend of the perennial search derives from the natural cycles of life and death, the seasons, the movements of the astral bodies and its symbolism could be extended almost endlessly. Methods of making this journey are those of dissociation from the usual mundane state. Some people indulge in self-imposed disciplines like fasting or other rigorous forms. There is the way of prayer or of meditation, while many people prefer a public form such as that enjoyed in the mystery plays or in the old shamanistic dance practices.

Having eliminated worldly identification the initiate enters the domain of terrors, the kingdom of the devil, the long night, the maya of Buddhism, the descent to the rescue of the soul, the battle with the powers of darkness. When these powers have been conquered the 'mystery' is complete and enlightenment achieved.

The idea of sacrifice as an appeasement of the natural forces frequently held strange and sinister aspects. Ancient Albanians worshipped the moon and had a man as their high priest. If anyone became possessed or insane, it was the duty of the priest to arrest him and bind him with sacred fetters. The victim was kept in luxury for a year, then anointed and sacrificed. He was pierced through the heart with a sacred lance and auguries were then declared to the public, drawn from the way he fell. The body was then taken to a sacred spot to be trampled on by the mob as a means of purification.

There was a time in England when annual human sacrifices were made to rivers to satisfy the water gods and prevent them from seeking other victims.

Living human beings were walled up inside castles and bridges when they were being built to ensure durability, as in the rhyme of "London Bridge is falling down, my fair lady". Ships are feminine because they were always dedicated to goddesses and a woman was always sacrificed as a gift by using her living body as one of the launching rollers. This is the origin of the present-day custom of women launching ships with champagne. The champagne replaces the blood of the original human sacrifice and is in itself a fertility symbol of prosperity and good wine harvest.

Even kings were not immune from sacrifice. In folklore it is con-

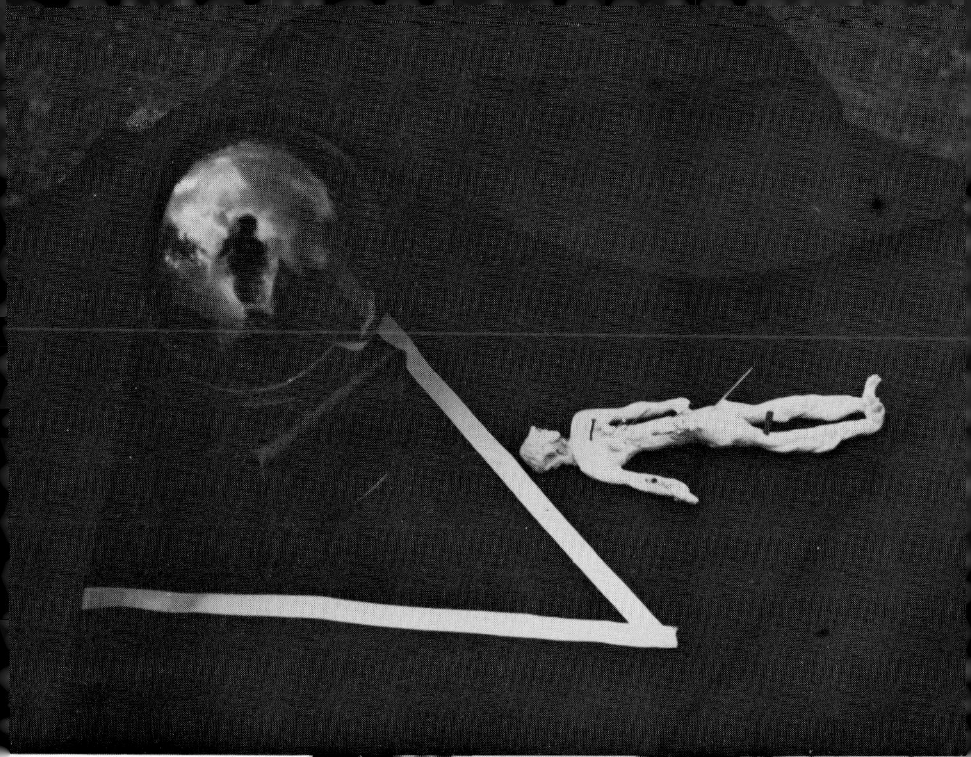

crystal ball inside its
angle representing the
ne of power and a clay
age stuck with pins.

witch mask from Zaire.

A witch's familiar can b imbued with special powers.

The traditional broomstick, or besom, outside a witch's house in Lincolnshire.

sidered most unlucky to kill a wren. The killer would at the very least thereafter break one of his own bones. The single exception to this taboo was the customary hunting of a wren on Christmas Eve. When the wren was caught it was fastened to the top of a pole with its wings spread out. It was carried to every house in the village and a protective feather left as a talisman. This was done to the chant of:

> We hunted the wren for Robin the Bobbin,
> We hunted the wren for Jack of the Can,
> We hunted the wren for Robin the Bobbin,
> We hunted the wren for every one.

This chant, with additional verses, has now become part of the folk singer's repertoire.

The custom was a clear case of substitution since the wren was regarded as king of the birds, and it was once usual to kill the human king in a ceremonial fashion before his natural powers failed. The king was the incarnation of a god upon whom the welfare of the tribe or nation depended. By killing him the divine power was released to take up its abode in the next king. The sacrifice was made at five- or seven-year periods when the divine principle was deemed to be at its strongest in the individual and it could then be released before its decline and consequent harm to the people. In later times a mock king or other substitute was found, and originally this was the golden-crested wren.

British coronation ceremonies show many remnants of customs which go back over a thousand years, such as the 'Recognition' and the anointing with oil to strengthen the king, which was its original purpose.

It has been intimated that many of the early kings of England were under the sway of witchcraft, the power of the old religion, despite their acceptance of Christianity. It is a curious fact that several of them held the crown or coronet in multiples of five- or seven-year spans. Making allowances for the method of dating coronations, it can be seen that William I reigned for twenty-one years, William II for thirteen, bringing him into the span of two periods of seven years. Henry I enjoyed thirty-five years rule or seven periods of five years, as did Henry II. The process repeats with striking regularity to at least the reign of Edward IV, 1461 to 1483, giving a period of just over three terms of seven years.

King William Rufus was killed by an arrow in the New Forest, and as he was supposed to be a witch, his entourage ran away for fear of becoming involved in counter-magic.

Kings, monks, soldiers, and gypsies are all buried wearing clothes, and this is in keeping with the old primitive idea of supplying needs for the journey. Swords and other regalia placed on a regal bier are another relic of a time when such articles would have been buried with the person.

The well known story of the origin of the premier Order of Chivalry in the world has overtones of witchcraft. It was instituted in the year 1348. King Edward III was dancing with the Countess of Salisbury when a garter dropped from her leg. The King picked it up and placed it around his own knee, rebuking the onlookers with the words in French, "*Honi soit qui mal y pense*". The popular modern way of expressing the phrase in English is 'evil to him who evil thinks', but a more exact translation would be, 'accursed be he who thinks ill of it'. The Order of the Garter was thus founded, and consisted originally of twenty-six members, or in other words two covens.

The point is that the badge of the well-to-do witch was a strip of green snakeskin backed with blue silk and with a silver buckle, worn as a garter. It may be supposed that the King was protecting the Countess who had inadvertently revealed that she was a member of the old religion.

Garter Knights of today have a broad blue ribbon worn diagonally from shoulder to hip, the garter itself being strapped below the left knee in Court dress, and it is of dark blue velvet edged with gold, and bears the motto in gold letters.

The insignia is also used as an army badge by some regiments such as the Royal Engineers. Another ancient order having mystical origins is the Scottish Order of the Thistle, founded by Achaius, King of the Scots, in the year 787. On the night before the battle in which he defeated Athelstan of England, Achaius saw a huge white cross in the sky. This cross is the central decoration in the Star and Badge of the Order, and is now known as Saint Andrew's Cross.

Incidentally, King Edward III reigned for fifty years, or a term of ten five-year periods.

7

CONVICTA ET COMBUSTA

The main historical objection to the witchcraft cult has always been that it is pagan and therefore heretical. This alleged anti-Christian element has been elaborated and frequently distorted over centuries and has resulted in terrible persecutions condoned by the Church, State, and laity alike.

It has been sometimes thought that the Church in one mighty exercise destroyed the phantoms of the old gods. Yet those divinities still held sway, linked inextricably with existence. Within the hearts, memories, and subconscious feelings they persisted, subject to change, but still perpetuating.

That the Church was aware of this was evidenced by periodic indignant attacks. Unable to vanquish the elves of the domestic hearth and the spirits of the forests, streams, hills, and plains, the Church baptized them and gave them new names and legends, and even admitted some into the Christian hierarchy.

Yet the pagans were by no means wholly converted, for their power was in the household, a domestic stronghold as insidious as the teachings from the temple, for it was blended to the feelings and inheritance of the folk. Fidelity to the old faith was preserved in race memory and in simple beliefs whose origins were forgotten or obscured by time, and even distorted at times to absurdity.

Some pursued their beliefs as a religion, some as a kind of natural science. Either form was forbidden by the Church. Punishments gradually increased in severity. What had been paid for in penances and fasting in the seventh century was paid for in Tudor and Stuart times by imprisonment or hanging, and by unofficial brutalities meted out by a populace terrified of the witches' power.

It was commonly believed in the sixteenth and seventeenth

centuries that witches were devil worshippers who formed the membership of a widespread organization. Several of those accused said they adored an alien spirit whom they called their Lord. Furthermore they said they met at stated intervals to perform curious religious rites.

Their descriptions pointed to the survival in many districts of ancient fertility cults driven underground by the advent of Christianity. When the king became converted it did not mean that his subjects automatically followed suit. Many people had confused ideas about the new faith, and in times of trouble were apt to revert to the old rites.

During the uneasy, troubled reign of King Stephen when the Norman barons were forcing people to build castles for them, it is recorded that a fairy girl and boy were found in Wolf Pit at Woolpit near Bury St Edmunds by harvesters. The children were crying and they were taken to the house of Sir Richard de Calne. They were of human appearance but had greenish-coloured skins and could not speak English. After they had been taught the language they told their hearers that they came from 'Saint Martin's Land' where the inhabitants were green like themselves. They claimed that the people there were Christians. In Saint Martin's Land it was always twilight and there was no sun or moon. One day the pair had followed the sound of bells through a cavern into the outside world and were unable to find their way back. Eventually the boy died, but the girl was baptized, she lost her green colour, and later married a man from King's Lynn.

The first recorded trial for witchcraft was in the reign of King John. "Agnes, the wife of Odo, accused Gideon of magic". The details are sparse, but Gideon was acquitted, being freed after undergoing trial by ordeal, the ordeal of grasping a red-hot iron.

In the year 578 the Council of Auxerre, a powerful ecclesiastical authority, issued a statement forbidding anyone "to masquerade as a bull-calf or a stag on the 1st of January or to distribute devilish charms".

The seventh Archbishop of Canterbury also reprobated these carnivals and practices of the old religion because in his book

Liber Poenitentialis he wrote, "If anyone at the Kalends of January goeth about as a stag or a bull-calf, that is, making himself into a wild animal and dressing in the skins of a herd animal, and putting on the heads of beasts; those who in such wise transform themselves into the appearance of a wild animal, let them do penance for three years, because this is devilish."

The faith of the horned hunting god and the moon-goddess was dying hard. Other 'devilish' practices were continuing too, such as prophecy, for Thomas of Erceldoune, better known as Thomas the Rhymer and who was born about the year 1230, foretold much of Scottish history including union with England. Thomas was believed to have gained his powers from the fairy folk, a supposition commonly accorded to those who could tell fortunes, cure illnesses, or call up invisible beings. In the true bardic tradition, Thomas the Rhymer has been credited with having written one of the earliest known metrical romances in English, the subject of which was the love of Tristan and Iseult.

The stories of high-born privileged witches usually begin with the affair of Dame Alice Kyteler of Kilkenny who was brought to trial in 1324. She was very rich and was accused of the usual denial of the Church, and of making sacrifices to the Devil, and of conducting rituals with a manifested demon in human form called Robin Artisson. She was also suspected of having done away with three of her husbands. In denying the bishop who brought the charges, Dame Alice showed her powerful influence by having him imprisoned. A curious judicial battle ensued, and eventually the lady fled to London and safety. One of her accomplices, Petronilla de Meath, was burned alive.

In 1376 Alice Perrers was charged with bewitching King Edward III but the charges were not pursued. The King died a year later.

A report made to King Henry IV in 1406 informed him that the diocese of Lincoln was "overrun by witches". During the same year in which Lincoln was 'overrun' the son of Robert III became King James I of Scotland. A Highland woman prophesied the course of his unhappy career right up to his murder at Perth in 1437. When the woman was asked what was the source of her knowledge, she replied that Hudhart had told her of these things. Hudhart was another name for the witch spirit known as Hudkin in the Netherlands and Germany, and has similarities with the Robin Goodfellow and Friar Rush of England.

The lot of kings during this period was indeed an uneasy one. Roger Bolingbroke who was a member of the Duke of Gloucester's entourage, was arrested on a charge of 'witching'. He was accused of using a wax image in a plot with the Duchess to secure her succession to the throne. He was hanged and the Duchess was given life imprisonment.

For her part in the plot against the life of Henry VI, Margery Jourdemain, the Witch of Eye, was burnt at Smithfield in 1441 as an accomplice of Eleanor of Gloucester. The Duchess of Bedford was cleared of a witchcraft charge in 1478. The charge was one of bewitching Edward IV by means of an image made of lead and described as being, "made lyke a man of arms, conteyning the lengthy of a mannes finger, and broken in the myddes and made fast with the wyre".

Richard III's accusation of Jane Shore was a deliberate use of her reputation as a witch, to enable him to seize power and dispose of his enemies. The reign of Henry VII saw the birth of the woman who was to become perhaps the most famous of English witches.

Ursula Sontheil was born near the Dropping Well, Knaresborough in July 1488. Her mother was Agatha Sontheil, sometimes called Southell, her father's name unknown. He rewarded Agatha for her company by giving her powers to heal or kill, to raise storms, to command men and animals, and to foresee and foretell the future.

Prior to this, Agatha was orphaned and destitute at fifteen and was forced to beg and exist on the charity of neighbours. One day a well-dressed stranger approached her and asked why she was so sad. Agatha explained her difficulties and they met again regularly until the young man seduced her. Then her lover revealed that he was no mere mortal, and promised that he would endow her with supernatural gifts.

Thereafter Agatha was often missing for days on end. Her

circumstances mysteriously improved and she now seemed to have enough money for her needs. The neighbours became very curious and their inquisitiveness annoyed Agatha so much that on one occasion she invoked a strong wind which caused the prying ones to quickly retreat to their own homes. Some of the envious and angry neighbours reported these matters to the local magistrates, whereupon Agatha was charged with witchcraft. She conducted her own defence so brilliantly that she was acquitted and henceforth left alone. Shortly after the birth of her daughter, Agatha retired to a convent where she died.

Ursula Sontheil was given into the care of the parish nurse. The child was unprepossessing, being mis-shapen, with distorted limbs, large goggling eyes, and a long crooked nose. Eventually she was sent to school where she amazed everyone by her brilliance. Although she was the star pupil, Ursula was inevitably the target for the cruelty of other children because of her freakish appearance. Ursula was not the daughter of a witch for nothing, and she was able to retaliate against her tormentors by use of the occult powers she had inherited. Persecutors found that they were punched and kicked and knocked down by invisible means. After several such manifestations the authorities decided that it was intolerable having a junior witch in the school, and Ursula was removed.

Nothing is known of her career after that until at the age of twenty-four she married Toby Shipton, of Shipton. Before very long she had gained a great reputation as a seer and rich and poor alike came from far and near to consult her about their lives and problems. As her fame spread she became known as Mother Shipton. She was not avaricious and her charges for consultation were very reasonable. Her maid however took bribes from people wishing for an audience, and though Ursula was aware of it, she took no action against the girl.

She once stated that the bridge across the River Ouse would be wrecked and that it could not be successfully rebuilt unless a stone from the Trinity Church was used in its construction. The bridge was destroyed by flood and when building the new replacement the masons found that each night their work had collapsed. Recalling the prophecy they then used some stones from the church steeple, which had blown down in a fierce gale. The bridge structure then remained firm.

In time Mother Shipton expanded her prophecies to include matters of political and historical import, and many of these prophecies are on record. She foretold many royal events as well as marvels of the future. Her forecasts are too many and detailed to enumerate, but are deservedly famous. As examples of foretelling modern matters, she mentioned the coming of such things as railways, cars, and radio. Like many other witches she foretold the date of her own death, which occurred in 1561.

By then she was greatly loved and respected and eventually a stone was erected to her memory at Clifton, near York. The inscription was:

> Here lies she who never ly'd,
> Whose skill so often has been try'd,
> Her prophecies shall still survive,
> And ever keep her name alive.

Such a memorial to a witch was most unusual, because the few reminders of witches that still survive are generally in the form of a cairn of stones to mark a place of degradation and execution, not one of praise.

Another person from Knaresborough with powers of divination was John Stewart. Records in York state that he was a schoolmaster who kept three bees under a stone which he could call out at will. He fed them with blood from his finger. Stewart was arraigned for witchcraft in 1510.

Meanwhile the pace of persecution in Europe was increasing all the time. Following on the issue of the Witch Bull of Pope Innocent, Inquisitor Cumanus had forty-one women burnt a year later in 1485. By about 1515 Inquisitor Remigius had put to death 900 people.

Clearly the respected Mother Shipton may be regarded as a white witch, and among the people at least, such distinctions were being made between the beneficial and the harmful practitioners of witchcraft. About 1527 two white witches were flourishing, William

Browne and Margaret Hunt. Margaret had learned her art from a Welsh witch called Mother Emet. They used a mixture of pagan spells and Christian prayers in their cures and also practised divination, as did Agnes Robson of Lincolnshire ten years later.

Henry VIII, never averse to execution in any form, had Elizabeth Barton put to death at Tyburn in 1534. She had been popularly known at the Holy Maid of Kent. He also had his favourite the Duke of Buckingham beheaded on Tower Hill in 1521, for consulting a wizard in order to seize the throne. Henry always claimed that Anne Boleyn practised witchcraft.

In 1538 Mabel Brigg was executed at York for practising the 'black fast', more of which later. Four years after that witchcraft was declared a civil offence in England and so became in law a felony, whereas in Scotland and the rest of Europe it remained heresy. The witch and those who consulted her were equally punishable. The clergy were not protected and the device of sanctuary did not operate. The Act seems to have had little enough effect for the belief in and practice of the Craft continued.

Another Act was passed in 1563 during the reign of Elizabeth. This statute made no reference to the usual consorting with 'familiars' and such like matters. It was really the extension of the death penalty to all those deemed to have caused death by witchcraft. The practice was now truly a felony, and the Act marked the real beginning of stringent official persecutions.

On 8th November 1576, Bessie Dunlop, the wife of Andro Jack of Lyne in Ayrshire, was accused of witchcraft. Her case was an odd one. She had made prophecies for people and had advised them how to find lost articles. Bessie told her accusers that she herself possessed no arts of her own and that she was enabled to do supernatural things only through the agency of one Thomas Reid. The Thomas Reid referred to had been dead for twenty-nine years, having been killed in the Battle of Pinkie fighting against the English army. Thomas had told Bessie Dunlop among other things, that he now belonged to elfland. And so a curious element of spiritualism entered the case. Although Bessie had a good reputation as a 'wise woman' and had cured many people of their ailments, this white witch was convicted and burnt to death. To those within the witch cult, it is revealing that Bessie's husband was called Andro, since this is an old witch name, and not to be confused with a corruption of Andrew.

The witch's familiar, the strange pet or pets kept by the practitioner, now began to play a more prominent part in the trials. At Windsor in 1579, Mother Dutton of Cleworthe Parish was said to have kept a fiend or spirit in the likeness of a toad. The creature lived in a border of green herbs. Mother Dutton fed her familiar with blood from her own thigh.

Old women had become popular targets for the witch hunters, and three years after the Act of 1563 the famous Chelmsford witch case was being judged. The trial lasted only two days and the prosecutor was the Reverend Thomas Cole. The case proved to be an important one, because it was used as a precedent of procedure for many later cases.

Elizabeth Francis, Agnes Waterhouse and Joan Waterhouse were the defendants. All three women lived in Hatfield Peverell, some five or six miles from Chelmsford. It was claimed that Elizabeth Francis had bewitched a small child and that she had exchanged her cat familiar for a cake given to her by old Mother Waterhouse. Elizabeth had been taught witchcraft by her grandmother, known as Mother Eve. She had been twelve at the time, and it was Mother Eve who had given her the cat as a familiar.

Agnes, Mother Waterhouse, was charged with bewitching a man to death. Her daughter Joan was likewise charged with bewitching a young girl. Mother Waterhouse was hanged, but her daughter Joan was found not guilty. Elizabeth Francis was given one year's imprisonment.

Elizabeth was singularly unfortunate for she was arrested again soon after her release and only released after another year. Then in 1579 she was charged again and hanged. Arraigned with her were three other women. Alice Noakes was hanged, also Ellen Smith, whose mother had been hanged in 1574. Margery Staunton was acquitted. During the time the unlucky Elizabeth Francis was undergoing her trials a man known as Old Rosimond was flourishing as the 'wise man' of Farnham and was leader of the local coven.

Essex seemed to have been a hotbed of witchcraft for in 1582 another thirteen women, all from the Saint Osyth district, were tried at Chelmsford.

Again familiars were mentioned in the proceedings. Ursula Kemp admitted possession of no less than four imps, two being cats, one was a lamb, and the last one a toad. Ursula was duly hanged. Elizabeth Bennett confessed to owning two imps and was also hanged. Two of the thirteen prisoners were reprieved, and the rest were freed, in the fearful knowledge that they could be prosecuted at any time. Alice Hunt of the same coven kept two ferrets as familiars, while Margery Sammon had two toads.

The familiar spirit of Alison Pearson who was burnt to death in Scotland in 1588 was her dead cousin William Sympson. Like Thomas Reid of twelve years earlier he declared when invoked that he came from elfland. During his human years he had been taken away by gypsies for a period of twelve years, and had learned many wonderful things.

Some of the tortures inflicted upon the accused were vile. In 1596 Alison Balfour was crushed by the arms in a vice for two days. Her husband, an old man of eighty, was 'pressed' under iron weights, while her son had his legs squashed to a pulp in the 'iron boots' and her seven-year-old daughter was tortured by thumbscrews.

Small wonder that all kinds of strange confessions were extracted under such conditions, and torture, along with crazy admissions from the near insane, were responsible for many of the odd stories concerning witchcraft.

Findings were arbitrary, some were freed, others imprisoned, and many were hanged and their bodies burnt, or were strangled at the stake and burnt, to have their individual file closed laconically with the words "*convicta et combusta*", convicted and burnt.

8

SOME MORE WITCHES

The revival of art and letters in Europe during the fifteenth and sixteenth centuries known as the Renaissance, with its spirit of intellectual inquiry, had given a challenge to the Church. Dominion was shaken to the extent that it was decided that the time had come for desperate measures.

Since historical effect is an ongoing process with gradual change, the Witch-Bull of 1484 was still fulfilling its purposes in the seventeenth century, albeit with modifications and for varying reasons.

The beginning of the century saw the hanging of Mother Jackson for bewitching in 1602, and closed the chapter of witchcraft persecution in Elizabethan England.

A year later James VI of Scotland became James I of England. He had already shown his diligence in pursuit of Scottish witches since 1567 such as in the affair of Agnes Sampson, called the Wise Wife of Keith. It was brought to light that she had been consulted concerning the illness of Isobel Hamilton and expressed her opinion that no cure could be made unless the devil could be raised. Agnes Sampson was a well educated, grave matron always composed and deliberate in speech.

Mr Hamilton refused to pay for such a cure as had been proposed and consequently the patient died.

It is just possible that the matter might have ended there and that Agnes would have continued to practise her healing arts, but unfortunately for her the deputy bailiff of Tranent near Edinburgh became suspicious of the night time activities of his young servant, Gilly Duncan.

Gilly Duncan had acquired a wonderful reputation for curing all manner of sickness and infirmity among the people. On learning this Seaton, her employer, tortured her to extract a confession of witchcraft. He twisted a cord around her head and crushed her fingers in a vice. He also examined her body for the telltale devil's mark. When Gilly confessed, Seaton handed her over to the authorities.

She was then asked to name her accomplices, and Agnes Sampson was one of those named. In all some seventy people were implicated, amongst them being Dame Euphane MacCalzean, the widow of a Senator of the College of Justice and a friend of the Earl of Bothwell, the Earl also being imprisoned. Others of this highly literate group were Doctor John Fian, a schoolmaster, and Barbara Napier, a woman of rank and sister-in-law of the Laird of Carschoggill. Alongside the educated members of the conclave were about thirty others of lower degree, including an old ploughman nicknamed Graymeal who acted as doorkeeper during their meetings.

A plot to harm the King was exposed in which attempts had been made to wreck the fleet in which he had previously sailed to marry Anne of Denmark. Many and fantastic were the confessions wrung from the prisoners who underwent the most horrible tortures.

They had raised storms, causing ships to sink, had used love-philtres, had held secret meetings in a church, gaining entry by merely blowing into the lock, and had enjoyed feasting and merriment of a diabolical nature, and had a knowledge of the intimate secrets of the King himself, and had made harmful waxen images.

Yet the jury dismissed the case.

Enraged by this, King James intervened and ordered Barbara Napier to be burnt at the stake and claimed her property for himself. The unfortunate acquittal jury were themselves tried for committing such an error of judgement.

Oddly enough Mrs Napier was set free after some time. But King James saw to it that Dame Euphane or Euphemia was burnt alive, as was Richard Graham, an associate of Barbara Napier. The King interrogated him personally as well as Agnes Sampson who was also burnt. The Earl of Bothwell escaped, probably through bribery, but most of the company were executed in 1591 and 1592.

Of the seventy Doctor Fian showed the most extraordinary courage, steadfastly refusing to confess even under the appalling tortures. His head was tied with a rope and savagely jerked about, his legs were crushed in the 'boots', an instrument like a large boot reaching almost to the knees and both legs put into it, when it could be tightened by several screws, and wedges hammered down between the knees. At the third such pressing Doctor Fian fainted. After being revived pins were stuck through his tongue in the presence of the King. He then said he would admit to whatever was alleged but would refuse to implicate others. Brought before the King again, Fian recanted all confession. For this defiance all his finger nails were torn off with pincers and needles were buried in his finger ends. Still he refused to confess and many more tortures followed, the boots being used again so that his legs were crushed to a pulp of blood and bone marrow.

Unable to gain the satisfaction of a confession his tormentors finally gave up. But death was inevitable and five weeks later Doctor Fian was burned on Castle Hill in Edinburgh.

The King had personally watched his tortures and had personally condemned him to death. He wasted no time in declaring his intentions in such matters concerning his English subjects. In 1604 he brought in even harsher laws stating in effect that all witches should be executed. In the Act of 1604 it became a felony to "consult, covenant with, entertain, employ, feed, or reward any evil and wicked spirit".

Witch trial records became filled with references to such creatures after that time, mainly because zealous interrogators included questions about familiars. Under pressure of fear and torture from the witch finders, the witches freely admitted the ownership of domestic pets. The keeping of any such pet was deliberately construed as evidence of trafficking with the Devil, and lurid and fantastic descriptions were recorded.

Where Ursula Kemp had confessed to having a black cat called Jack, a grey cat called Titty, a black lamb called Tyffin, and a black toad called Pigin, at another Chelmsford trial the young son of

Ellen Smith had revealed that his mother kept three imps. By such admission it was soon felt necessary to prove guilt by such possessions, even if only some humble insect such as a bee or a fly could be included in the allegations. This at least had a form of precedent if we recall John Stewart's blood-nourished bees.

In 1606 Ralph Milner was more fortunate than Mother Jackson four years earlier. He was arraigned at Richmond for telling fortunes as a witch. His lenient sentence was merely to be ordered to make confession at Muker Church. Even after this brush with the law he continued his practices until he died a natural death.

Isabel Grierson was hanged and burnt at Edinburgh in 1607 for shape-changing, having been seen entering a house in the guise of a cat. Four years later Susan Beaumont and Mary Sykes were accused on similar charges.

Whereas Elizabeth Cooke was cleared of witchcraft at Thirsk in 1611, the following year brought a case as notorious as anything that had ever occurred at Chelmsford.

Mrs Elizabeth Southerne, a woman of eighty who lived in the Forest of Pendle, was arrested. She was known locally as Old Demdike, and confessed to having been a witch since 1560. In 1565 she had been joined in her practices by Mrs Ann Whittle, otherwise known as Old Chattox. Later on they were joined by their daughters, Elizabeth Device and Ann Redfearne, along with several other relatives and friends.

The association attracted some attention and brought the arrest of Old Demdike in 1612. Under questioning by the magistrates she implicated Old Chattox and her own grand-daughter. All three were committed to Lancaster Castle. Alison Device the grand-daughter, confessed to having lamed Robert Nutter, implicating Old Chattox in the subsequent spelling to death of the man.

Because of their joint association, Old Demdike, Elizabeth Device, and Ann Redfearne were also charged with the same offence. The arrest of the last two and seven others was because of a meeting they held in Malkin Tower in Pendle Forest. At this meeting they planned to rescue the two old women and Alison from Lancaster Castle gaol. The plan was to kill the gaoler and blow up the castle. This odd meeting was concluded with feasting and jollity.

Some unknown person reported the content of the meeting to the authorities with the result that nine arrests were made, and twelve others escaped into hiding.

James Device, twenty-one-year-old son of Elizabeth, and his nine-year-old sister Jennet both gave evidence against their mother, as did Alison. Eventually Elizabeth herself made a full confession.

The hopes of James Device for leniency for his co-operation were dashed when his little sister gave evidence against him, saying that he kept a familiar to bewitch people to death. Ann Redfearne was at first acquitted on a plea of inconclusive evidence. This verdict proved so unpopular with the many spectators that to appease their rage a new charge was brought and she was found guilty.

James Device confessed that he had gone to church in order to receive the communion to keep the wafer he was given, to use later for magical purposes. This he had done at the bidding of Old Demdike.

Old Chattox and her daughter Ann were hanged. So was Elizabeth Device, James, and Alison, and also Mrs Nutter, widow of Robert who had been bewitched to death. Alice Nutter, unlike the others, was a wealthy woman, and she was charged with killing a man called Henry Mytton. Old Demdike cheated the gibbet, for she died in prison.

Altogether ten of the Lancashire witches were hanged. Several had admitted ownership of familiars. What had really led to their apprehension in the first place was that both of the principal families had often advertised locally that they were responsible for all the unexplained deaths in the neighbourhood. There was rivalry for custom between the two factions, and they imagined that such rumours would enhance their reputations. Then when the law intervened the rivals had joined forces in a futile attempt to repel the common enemy.

The Demdike and Chattox clans discovered to their cost that the evidence of witches was accepted against other alleged witches, but that an accused speaking on his own or her own behalf was accorded little credibility.

To expose family quarrels or seek redress from the courts was in many instances to invite disaster. A certain Margaret Barclay was not on good terms with her husband's brother John and his wife Janet. They had accused her of theft from them. This rankled with Margaret Barclay so much that she took her sister-in-law to the church court over the matter. There the two women were told to shake hands and become reconciled. Margaret declared that she could not forgive her in-laws for the slight on her character.

John Dein, the brother-in-law, was a sailor. He set out on a voyage to France accompanied by the owner of the ship, Andrew Train or Tran, who was also the provost of Irvine. Margaret Barclay was heard to curse her brother-in-law, the ship, and all in her.

This was unfortunate because some time later John Stewart, who was a wandering beggar and spaeman or fortune-teller, called at the house of the provost and said that the ship had been lost in a gale off the Cornish coast.

Later on his story was confirmed by two sailors who had survived the wreck. Margaret Barclay and John Stewart were immediately suspected of bewitching. Stewart was arrested first on a charge of precognition, and Margaret was charged with witchcraft. Stewart claimed that she had asked for his aid. He had visited her at a deserted house where with a woman called Isobel Insh she was making wax images of the ship and the provost and clay images of others in the crew. On this evidence Isobel Insh was tortured into confession. She was then imprisoned in the church belfry from which she escaped on to the roof. She then slipped from the roof and died five days later from her injuries. Her eight-year-old daughter had also been seized and questioned until she gave evidence against her elders.

John Stewart was kept fettered and under constant guard, but still contrived to strangle himself to death just before the trial, by using the cords from his bonnet.

Margaret Barclay was tortured by being put into stocks and

heavy iron bars being increasingly added to her legs. When she could stand the pain no longer, she made a confession which implicated yet another woman, Isobel Crawford, who was given the same kind of torture. Both were then convicted and burnt.

When Edward Fairfax charged six women with witchcraft in 1621 he attempted to describe their familiars. He said Margaret Wait had a curious, deformed creature with many feet which was as big as a cat, black and with long rough hair. It is no surprise to learn that he was unable to put a name to this oddity. Mrs Wait's daughter had a white cat with black spots and called Inges. An old woman called Jennet Dibble also had a black cat, known as Gibbe. Her daughter Margaret Thorpe displayed originality in possessing a yellow bird known as Tewhitt, which could have been an owl, a lapwing, or a peewit. Elizabeth Fletcher was not known to have a familiar and the sixth woman charged was not even known by name to Fairfax, though he declared she had owned a familiar for over twenty years, a white cat called Fillie.

In that year Elizabeth Sawyer, the witch of Edmonton, was hanged. She was a humble pedlar of brooms and the accusations made against her came from neighbours as reprisals for her harsh words at their doorsteps when they refused to buy her wares. They claimed that misfortune always followed such encounters.

The serious dangers inherent in consorting with witches was forcibly pointed out to Margaret Wallace in Glasgow in 1622. Her crime was friendship with Christian Grahame, a known witch.

At Doncaster in 1623 Jane Blonely was accused of bewitching to death Mrs Frances Craven, and in the same year Elizabeth Creasey was given one year's imprisonment for bewitching cattle. The executions of at least fifty people accused of witchcraft are recorded for the years 1603 to 1625, the reign of James I of England.

Charles I inherited the belief in the divinity of kingship. Until his beheading in 1649 there was no relief for the witches of Britain. At least Isobel Young, strangled and burnt in 1629, had undergone such processes of law as were available, unlike Old Wife Green who was burnt alive at Pocklington by a mob in 1631, before the law could intervene. The Pocklington parish records show that the blacksmith's wife Petronal Haxley was legally executed in the market square.

About 1634 a boy called Edmund Robinson was gathering 'bullees' or wild plums in the notorious Pendle Forest when he should have been tending his father's cattle. He saw two greyhounds and tried to course a hare with them, but they would not run. As he was about to hit them with a stick they suddenly transformed themselves into a woman and a boy. The woman was Dame Dickenson, wife of a neighbour. She offered money to Edmund to say nothing of the matter, but he refused the taint of such an unholy bribe. Dame Dickenson then changed her boy companion into a horse and rode off on it, forcing Edmund to accompany her. They rode to a large barn and inside were several other people who were pulling on halters. This activity magically preduced a rustic feast of meat, bread, butter, and milk.

Much frightened by his marvellous experiences, young Edmund escaped and reported to his father. Robinson senior instructed the boy to attend various churches in the district to identify the witches among the congregations. The father had given evidence against witches before in 1613, and knew how easy it usually was to secure convictions.

All told, young Edmund selected thirty people for the usual accusations, and seventeen were tried and found guilty. The justices showed some unease about the whole matter and referred it to the King's Council. On further investigation the Bishop of Chester discovered that the senior Robinson had offered to drop accusations against any one of his victims if they would buy him off.

It was then that Edmund Robinson became frightened and admitted that the whole business was a lie, a blatant corruption in which his father hoped to gain monetary profit.

Those prisoners who had not died under prison conditions were then released, and among them was Jennet Device who had figured in the Demdike-Chattox trials years before. Robinson senior was sent to the Westminster Gatehouse prison.

The Civil War did nothing to abate witch-hunting, if anything the turmoil exacerbated it. It saw the emergence of Matthew Hopkins, the infamous witch-finder. He was a failed lawyer who moved from Ipswich to Manningtree in Essex.

No one felt certain about the eventual outcome of the Civil War. The Roundheads stood for complete Protestantism, and witches to them represented a threat to republicanism and God. Catholics were to them an obvious enemy, witches were more subtle, and had to be discovered.

Sensing the possibility of a lucrative career, Hopkins set himself up as a witch-finder. For his first victim he chose a one-legged old woman called Elizabeth Clarke.

Through all of the cases since about 1566 a pattern had emerged. Familiars and witch marks had become standard items of evidence, young children were allowed to indulge their imaginations in the name of acceptable evidence. The involvement of others named under confession was taken as definite proof of guilt and complicity.

Matthew Hopkins utilized all of these standard features for his own advantage. He also introduced methods of torture which would leave his victims unmarked but still result in confession. He had eighty-year-old Elizabeth searched for witch marks and obtained authority from the magistrates to conduct further investigations.

Then he kept the old woman awake for several nights on the pretext of watching for visiting imps or familiars, but this was really one of his methods of torture. For sanction concerning imps or familiars, Hopkins used the book entitled *Demonology*, written by King James.

He and his assistants swore they had observed four familiars while watching the old woman. They were in the forms of a white dog, a greyhound, a polecat, and an unidentified black imp. The confession extracted from Elizabeth Clarke provided five other victims. Proliferation of success caused Hopkins to employ two full time assistants, John Stearne and Mary Phillips.

The number of their suspects grew to thirty-two, all of whom were remanded to Chelmsford County Sessions. Elizabeth Clarke was hanged for "entertaining evil spirits". It could not have helped her case that it was well known that her mother had also been hanged as a witch.

Four of the other accused died in gaol, and of the remaining twenty-eight, fifteen were hanged. Encouraged by his success, Hopkins spread his activities, to become the scourge of eastern England, and he gave himself the title of Witch-Finder General.

He and his two assistants became adepts at their trade. They would sometimes force their sleepless prisoners to run about in a room until utterly exhausted. Another technique they used was that of 'swimming' a suspect, throwing the trussed victim into a pond or stream to see if they sank. When they searched the bodies of alleged witches for marks they used pricking instruments, and after operating in Essex, Hopkins turned his attentions to Norfolk, Suffolk, and later to the counties of Cambridge, Northampton, Bedford, and Huntingdon, by which time he was employing four prickers in addition to his other staff.

It had long been supposed that every witch had an area of flesh insensitive to pain. Sometimes spikes were used that had hollow handles into which the spikes would retract. In any case Hopkins and his helpers could always find alleged witch marks, and had plenty of ways of witch-finding.

In fourteen months Hopkins sent more witches to their deaths than any other witch hunter in 160 years of continued persecution. Meanwhile the hunt went on in the rest of the country.

In Beverley Elizabeth Roberts was charged with shape-changing, tormenting John Greencliffe in the likeness of a bee and a cat. Four women were charged at Heptonstall in 1646, and Isabella Billington and her husband were executed at Pocklington in 1648.

It is perhaps incredible to us how people persisted in practices of witchcraft in times when it was so obviously dangerous. Yet here and there they got away with it.

William Lilly was a seer, astrologer, and white witch. He was a friend of many well-known Puritans and members of the Cromwellian Long Parliament. Yet he carried on his witchcraft in the heart of London without any attempt at secrecy. He had walked to the city from Derby when a poor boy, and stayed to make his fortune. He foretold the Great Plague and the Great Fire of London, and many other things, and was also a healer who often treated people without accepting a fee.

At the same time the ease of making charges was amply demonstrated when the case of Joan Peterson, the witch of Wapping was brought. She was revered by the common people for her healing powers and her ability to combat black witchcraft. The undoing of this 'wise woman' was engendered by some gentlemen who wanted to murder a woman who stood between themselves and a sizeable legacy.

Joan refused to enter such a plot despite the offer of £100, in those times a lot of money. The conspirators, realizing they were dealing with an honest person, grew afraid that she might expose them. In order to silence her they brought charges against both her and Mrs Levingstone, their intended victim.

The trial was a mockery, false witnesses were brought and the jury intimidated. Joan Peterson was hanged on 12th April 1652.

Isobel Emott was more fortunate at Leeds in the following year, for the judge acquitted her, refusing to believe that she had bewitched some cattle. A salutary lesson concerning the ingratitude of patients was given to Yorkshire witch Anne Greene, for despite the fact that she had cured him of a severely painful earache, John Tatterson reported her for witchcraft. She was let off, and it is not known if she continued her medical work.

Still in Yorkshire, Thomas Jefferson of Sheffield was accused with his wife and Mary Butler of digging up corpses in order to practise necromancy. He was also charged with bewitching to death Mary Almond in 1657. Strangely enough, Thomas was released, but his female partners were executed.

The British throne had been regained by Charles II by the time the extraordinary case of Isobel Gowdie was heard in Scotland in 1662. As a case it was an absolute gift to the witch hunters, because in four separate confessions given voluntarily she made what amounted to a résumé of just about every belief concerning witchcraft ever held. She had made a pact with the Devil in Auldearne Church in 1647 and been given his mark. She had ridden to sabbats on broomsticks and belonged to a coven of thirteen. On occasion she had turned herself into a cat, and sometimes a jackdaw. There were numerous spells and demonic graces which she freely uttered. Her coven performed various activities such as storm raising, and each member had a personal familiar, all of which she named.

Perhaps the most singular part of this free recital was that concerning matters of elfland, for there had been little if any mention of the fairy kingdom for many years. Isobel related how at Lammas of 1659 she and other witches had gone to Dounie Hills. There a hillside opened to admit them to a large brightly lit room. They met the fairy king and queen and saw fairies or elves manufacturing arrow heads or elf-bolts. She herself had killed William Brown with one of these weapons, and had attempted the life of the Laird of Park.

She implicated several others in her confessions, Margaret Wilson, Bessie Wilson, Bessie Hay, and Jane Mairten who she declared was maiden of the coven, John Young being the officer of the coven. As a final act of self-condemnation Isobel Gowdie stated that she deserved to be tortured and put to death. Her wish was granted.

That shape-changing remained a popular art was revealed in 1663 when an old woman called Julian Coxe was executed on the evidence of a huntsman who said that a hare he was chasing had suddenly turned into her.

The dismal catalogue of persecution went on throughout the seventeenth century. Amy Dunny and Rose Callender hanged at Saint Edmondsbury in 1664, their case sparked off by their refusal to buy some herrings. Ann Foster and Ann Armstrong, 1673, Bessie Weir at Paisley in 1678. At Exeter in 1682 Susan Edwards, Mary Trembles, and Temperance Lloyd were hanged, as usual, after forced confession.

Gradually however the climate of opinion had been changing, particularly amongst the highly literate. Between 1584 and 1677, eleven books had been published which expressed varying degrees of scepticism about evidence offered at witch trials. This literature must have had some effect on a few members of the magistracy. There were of course several books, pamphlets, and broadsheets arguing a case for existing methods.

To bring to a close the bloody record of official practice with regard to witchcraft in England Alice Molland was hanged at Exeter in March, 1685. There were other cases brought in England, but no more executions occurred. In 1712 Jane Wenham, the witch of Walkerne, was tried. The jury found her guilty, but the judge managed to save her life. Thereafter Colonel Plummer of Gilston in Hertfordshire gave her his protection.

Then the last case taken before an English court was in 1717, when Jane Clarke and her son and daughter appeared on various charges including the old favourite of shape-changing. The accused were pricked and searched for witch marks, and underwent the swimming test. Despite all this and twenty-five witnesses, the jury set the prisoners free, making it clear that the courts would no longer act automatically in such cases.

This encouraged the mobs to take matters into their own hands on many occasions, but it also led to the repeal of previous Witchcraft Acts, a new one being substituted in 1736, aimed now at fraudulent practices carried out under the guises of "witchcraft, sorcery, enchantment or conjuration".

The number of alleged witches officially put to death up to this time will never be known. Hundreds of cases were brought, many of them on flimsy, trivial, or ridiculous evidence.

Yet there is no doubt that large numbers of people were engaged in witchcraft in Britain.

9

FOUR SABBATS TO BELTANE

To early man the supernatural world was real and awesome. Great dependence was put upon propitiatory worship of the gods. There was also still some reliance upon telepathic communication as well as on articulated speech. The animal kingdom still retains this gift or sense of telepathic communication. To look into a field of brussels sprouts and to see the sudden explosion of pigeons rushing up into the air as one bird at the intrusion, yet no audible cry of warning has been given, is to witness telepathy in action.

The realization of man that he was involved with various cyclic rhythms such as night and day, the seasons, the movement of tides, affected his life. Knowledge of the irregularities like variations of temperature, the feel of sun and rain and wind, also affected him powerfully because he was unable to determine the causes of such phenomena.

This led to attempts to define and prognosticate conditions, for it was observed that these conditions also influenced the vegetation necessary to existence.

By imitation it was thought that through the very similarity of things there could be produced a similarity of effect. From this primitive mimetic theory eventually sprang the medieval theory of medical practice know as the doctrine of signatures.

On this theory the witches based their own closely guarded secrets of healing. And by dramatic imitation or pleading, plants and animals could be increased, rain could be caused, and by extension people could also be worked upon.

Vibrations of various degrees were found to have power. Simple things like sowing by hand required a regular striding motion and a rhythmic cast to ensure an even crop. Ideas similar to this are with us today, such as talking to plants, whistling for wind, and the association of ideas contained in the idea that 'if I take my umbrella, or raincoat, it won't rain'. There is a kind of inverted logic contained in this mental hedging of bets.

The fertility rites were for the increase of herds and for the growing of food, and not as is sometimes supposed, for an orgiastic gratification of human sexual desires. Certainly the desperately impotent husband or barren wife could receive individual treatment, but the true purpose of general rites was for obtaining food, since even then it was realized that the ability to procreate human life exceeded the ability to sustain it.

So witchcraft was a nature cult linked with hunting and husbandry, the progress of crops through sowing, nurturing, harvesting, and garnering. This meant that each season required its own special regard, along with the other special agents of climate such as wind, rain, heat, cold, and the sun and the moon.

Therefore the four sabbats of Candlemas or 2nd February, May Eve or the last night in April, Lammas on the night of 1st August, and Hallow Eve are all linked with agricultural and hunting seasons. They also coincide with stages of man's reincarnation.

The mating times of animals are reflected too in the dates of some of the big festivals of witchcraft. Such celebrations as those of Lupercalia for protection from wolves and also for fruitfulness, on 15th February were the times when originally devotees would clothe themselves in animal skins. Some also wore masks, and certain trees would be hung with images for the casting of spells.

The first god of the man was the great horned hunter called by different names in different places. Early cave drawings of the horned god are to be found in the Pyrenees. Such traces of the magical fertility cult can be seen in several European caves and are drawings of the Aurignacian period of cave-dwellers. There are imprints of human hands and drawings of animals and masked men.

A carving in stone of the horned god once lay on the site of the Notre Dame Cathedral, and an engraving of him on reindeer bone is to be seen in the British Museum. The British names of the horned hunter have been passed down to us as Cernunnos, which is Latinized Celtic meaning 'horned one', and as Hob or Hobin, being variants of Robert and Robin, and also as Old Hornie, Herne the Hunter, Hobgoblin, and Old Nick.

At Abbot's Bromley in Staffordshire an ancient horn dance is still performed at the fair in July and during the wakes in September. The horns or antlers used are kept in a church dedicated to Saint Nicholas. There are about 400 churches so named in England, ostensibly to this patron saint of Russia, children, seafarers, and merchants. His date of celebration was transferred from 6th December to Christmastide, the ceremony of making gifts being continued and the name being popularized as Father Christmas and Santa Claus, the latter being a Dutch corruption.

It will be recalled that Saint Nicholas is none other than Old Nick, the annual bringer of gifts by reindeer. The commercial activity of allowing children to ask for gifts from Father Christmas is a remnant of the old practice of presenting the children ceremonially to the horned god of the witches.

The May tree customs which are so universal spring from tree worship. Once, a May tree was planted before practically every dwelling in the country. When and where this was impractical, people rose after midnight on May Eve to bring branches from the woods, adorn them with flowers, and fasten them to house doors. The men who left the branches were known as the Maybirchers. These customs brought to the village the blessing which the tree spirit could bestow. Then the English village Maypole became a permanent erection instead of being renewed annually. It was usually made from a fir trunk and on celebration days had to be dressed with green foliage and with flowers to show that it represented a living tree. It was thought that the god or spirit of vegetation took up abode in the boughs.

Tree spirits usually occupied one tree temporarily before moving on to another, which is partly why some groves were held to be sacred. Even now many a farm or country plot has a tree that is never touched because it seems to have some venerable merit of its own.

The spirit often became personified in much the same way as animals had been. Customs were born in which a man was covered in green foliage and known variously as Green George or Jack-in-the-Green. His function was to bring the life of the forest to bless the cultivation of the corn fields.

There was much dancing attached to these celebrations, with leading figures involved like the May King, Queen of the May, or the Whitsuntide King. The Queen of the May was a virgin who held her title for the year unless she married during that time. A new maiden was elected each year. Another goddess of fertility in Celtic times was Brigit. The anti-pagan campaigns of the Church converted her into Saint Bridget, taking away the pagan aspects of her predecessor.

Not only did the Church sanctify some of the old witch gods and goddesses, but also promoted rival miracles such as that of the legend of the famous Glastonbury Thorn, the tradition being that about the year A.D. 60 Saint Joseph of Arimathea arrived in Britain to preach. On Wearyall Hill he stuck his staff into the ground. Forthwith it sprouted and flowered, continuing to blossom twice a year ever since, at Christmas and in spring. The ruined abbey at Glastonbury was said to have been founded by Joseph, but actually it was founded in A.D. 601 according to the *New Standard Encyclopaedia* of 1932.

In some of the southern counties of England the custom of 'crying the neck' was performed until recent times. It had similar rites to those celebrated in ancient Egypt and dedicated to Cairis as the spirit of harvest.

An old man was sent into the fields to choose a bundle of the best ears of corn. This bundle was tied in a special way, becoming the neck of wheat. After the harvest the men and women gathered in a circle around the old man who stooped with the 'neck' to the ground. To a chant of 'the neck' the men removed their hats, likewise stooping to the ground. Still chanting, they raised their hats over their heads as the neck of wheat was raised. This stooping and standing was repeated three times, and then the chant became a faster one of 'Wee-yen' followed by 'Way-yen', also done three times in the same manner as before. The merriment then began with the 'neck' being run to the farmhouse. Some placed a 'kern-baby' of barley straw opposite the gate of a wheat field to avert storms.

Britain is particularly rich in such fertility lore, including things like tying protective hazel twigs round a cow's neck and making corn dollies in the shape of birds to be stuck on the tops of hayricks, this last having connections with the weathercock. Even the builder's 'topping out' ceremony was originally, like the ship-launching rite, a placatory gesture to the gods.

Although Easter became the ecclesiastical festival of the Resurrection, the name was derived from Eostre, the Anglo-Saxon goddess of spring. The date of Easter Day has varied through the ages. Once, Easter fires were lit all over Europe. Dedicated to Beltane, from Bel the Gaelic sun god and Tein the fire god, they were lit on 30th April to mark the renewal of the power of fire and the coming of summer, and were attended by jollity and feasting. Cattle were driven through the fire and men also leapt through it to gain the virtues of its purification.

A ritual cake was made and divided by lots and the unlucky person who received a certain portion was shunned for some time, and was once probably sacrificed to the flames. Now Christianized in the 'hot-cross bun', such cakes never went mouldy and were good for internal troubles if ground up and mixed with hot water, the same applying to the special cakes baked on Christmas Eve.

As the hearth was the sacred abode of the household gods and fire was also sacred, it was customary to keep the fire going all year, then on certain holy days of the pagan calendar new fire was made by use of a spindle set in an oak log. Only then could all the household fires be put out or the new 'needfire' would not ignite. When it did, all the fires were re-lit from it. To drive cattle through the ashes of the sacred needfire was to prevent murrain, a deadly and infectious disease in animals.

If a man failed to make a needfire it was considered an unpardonable sin. The Yule was an Anglo-Saxon fire celebration at what is now Christmas time. To keep a piece of the Yule log burnt then, was to protect the household from fire all the year. But to give anyone fire from your own house on New Year's Day was to invite a death in that house within a year, and a person was not allowed to poke your fire until he had been a friend for seven years. Elderly people in Holland preserve a remnant of this custom, for if they poke the fire in your presence it means an acceptance of your friendship. The setting fire to the pudding on Christmas Day is another relic of Yuletide fire worship. In northern countries the sun was regarded as a beneficent deity from whom proceeded all life and the sacred fire which defeated evil. Worshippers strengthened its power by ceremonial bonfires and by beating on metal and dancing sunwise or deosil to scare away the demon which caused eclipses.

Deosil or deseal, meaning right-hand circuiting, is the most universal belief connected with the sun, known long before clocks and the expression 'clockwise' now so commonly used. Games and dances were usually performed in this direction, for in all primitive religions this was the 'good' direction. Widdershins was the opposite direction performed for 'bad' purposes, and brought misfortune. To run widdershins three times round the church was to see the Devil look out of the porch.

Stirring of food mixtures such as jam should always be done deosil, millstones were set to run the same way, and the rich gentleman passed the port wine in the same manner. Wells were also built deosil.

All bonfire and firework festivities, including the Guy Fawkes excuse, all derive from the ancient idea of fire or sun worship.

The festival of Samhain fell on 31st October. As the pagan year was divided into two main periods of summer and winter, with subdivisions, and winter started on 1st November, it was one of those periods heralded by kindling of needfires and lighting of ceremonial bonfires. May Day Eve and Midsummer Eve also saw the fires blazing.

Lighted brands were carried round fields to make the crops grow, and special cakes were eaten. Many of the Samhain rites were gradually transferred to other winter festivals and the Yule Feast or Christmas, Twelfth Night and New Year's Day, all show signs of ancient sun and fire worship in the Yule log, candles, Christmas tree 'fairy' lights, and so on.

But Samhain or Hallowe'en was the great feast of the dead and the Christian Church has preserved the tradition in the twin feasts of All Saints and All Souls. At Samhain the barriers between this world and the next fell, the dead could return to visit their relations, and fairies and witches were much in evidence.

The notion of capturing the virtues of the sun through fire is inherent in all the uses of symbolic torches, such as that of the Olympic Games. On Easter Morning it was once customary to place a vessel with water in it where the first rays of the sun would strike it. If the reflected light appeared to tremble in the water the season would be a rainy one. If the light was steady, a good year would ensue. And if the Midsummer Eve fire was not lit, the least that would happen would be that the apple crop would fail. The smoke from this fire should be allowed to pass over the crops in the fields. On Easter Sunday it was said that the sun danced or spun for joy at its rising and setting.

The burning of candles around a corpse helped to keep away evil spirits. To bury the dead with the feet to the east or sunrise is a custom far older than Christianity, being a relic of sun worship. The Christian idea is that the summons of the Last Judgment will come from that direction. To light a candle directly from the fire in the hearth was to invite poverty.

A good harvest could be ensured by burning blackthorn and throwing the ashes over the first spring sowing. 25th December was originally regarded as the birthday of the sun. The ashes from the Yule log burnt on the fire on Christmas Eve were collected and placed under the milk bench in the cellar or the dairy to keep evil away from the yield. If however the log had not burned away the ashes could not be removed until another fire had burned, and on no account must fire be taken out of the house between Christmas Eve and New Year's Day. A candle or lamp left burning all night on Christmas Eve was to prevent death in the household during the year. In some northern counties such as Yorkshire many grocers used to give their customers a free candle for this purpose, and some joiners sent a gift of a Yule log to their good customers.

If the sun shone brightly on the apple trees on Christmas morning it presaged a good crop. On Candlemas, 2nd February, all the Christmas decorations were burnt. In Nottinghamshire this was known as Blaze Day, and the belief there was that if "Candlemas Day be fine and clear, we shall have winter all the year".

'Smoking the Fool' the centuries-old Haxey Hood custom in Lincolnshire.

Corn dollies, traditionally made from the last sheaf o the harvest and a relic of ancient fertility beliefs.

Water divining was one of the skills expected of the wise man or woman.

Balefire was, and is, that fire used at actual witchcraft meetings and festivals. Needfire was, strictly speaking, that used for domestic or lay purposes, although balefire is sometimes referred to as needfire, since it is also needed. Balefire is also called wildfire or elf-fire.

Wherever possible balefire was produced by some sort of spontaneous combustion, such as by the use of a magnifying glass, rather than by mechanical means such as striking flints, or wood friction. In this way the fire was 'wild' because it was produced directly from the sun, instead of being tamed by man. It was also elf-fire because of this same direct magical quality. We are all familiar with the saying, 'to spread like wildfire'.

Balefire used at witch Sabbats was traditionally kindled from nine different kinds of wood: rowan, apple, elder, holly, pine, cedar, juniper, poplar, and dogwood.

10

FAMILIARS AND OTHER ANIMALS

Although witchcraft is a universal cult, and certainly throughout Europe its forms were broadly the same, certain aspects were emphasized in different areas; the aspect of familiars in England, for example, where many epithets were given to them such as imp, bunting, dandiprat, spirit, devil, fiend, little master, puckril, mommet, and other names. In America the most popular title given to a familiar was that of spectre.

Many witches have kept and do keep familiars. Usually small animals, they could assist in various forms of divination for their owners. Animals can be observed for certain signs of behaviour giving prognostications, perhaps best known in the field of weather forecasting. They could also pick out forecasts by selecting slips of paper, or other materials.

There is also another use for the familiar. When a witch owns a pet a deep emotional rapport can be established. The pet can absorb from its owner what might be called a powerful psychic 'charge'. The animal can convey this charge, beneficent or otherwise, to another person.

This is an occult extension of the better known activities in regard to pet animals. Dogs are trained for retrieving, as shepherds, to do police work such as sniffing out drugs or discovering corpses, and are trained to guard premises and attack intruders. I well remember travelling in a ship to the port of Adabiya during the Suez crisis. On board were fourteen R.A.F. police dogs with their two handlers, a sergeant and a corporal. Twelve of the dogs were trained to kill, and two were trackers only. The understanding between these animals and their handlers was complete and truly remarkable.

Where these dogs were absolutely obedient to commands to kill or follow a trail, the witch-owned animal can be utilized in a more subtle manner, and the victim or the patient can become the recipient of a full psychic charge from the witch in question.

The fact that the original fertility cults were involved with shamans and other leaders dressed in animal costumes is another factor in perpetuating ideas of animal worship and familiarity. There are indeed cases of witch mediums evoking spirit elementals in the shape of animals. It is these factors which have contributed to the stories about, and the misunderstanding of witch familiars.

Much nonsense has been recorded in witch trial reports concerning the familiar. It has usually been said that this was a form of demon, often in some monstrous animal shape. Some of the records also recognized the familiar as being some pet of the witch in normal guise but possessed of evil powers. Apart from occasionally trying to describe fantastic creatures born of witch-finders' minds and other interested accusers, some records detail many real pets owned by alleged witches. Even so, several of those listed might seem curious, for among the dogs and cats listed there were also toads, bees, and even flies.

The legends of lycanthropy and shape-changing have some basis in fact. Old stories of witches being seen in the form of animals such as cats and hares and so on, are legion, and invariably relate how when the witch returned to human shape, he or she bore the wounds inflicted on the animal. Sometimes such occurrences must have been due to coincidence, sometimes an imagined happening, frequently pure invention, yet sometimes an elemental spirit would be involved.

Where an elemental had been deliberately invoked by a witch, the wound would be the result of a powerful repercussion, either the violent fear of the witness or victim, or the counter spell of some adept, rebounding through the elemental and back on to its originator.

Astral projection is a method by which a skilled occultist can mount an attack. Recoil is however an attendant danger to the operator, and can occur if the intended recipient is knowledgeable in such matters, or can engage the assistance of another occultist.

On the other hand, when the victim has no such aid and is haunted by an elemental, the lessening of vitality and ensuing illness give rise to the symptoms of vampirism.

This method of astral travelling was known to the old witches as 'sending the fetch'. Vampires, werewolves, and the incubus and the succubus are examples of such astral projections, the incubus being a male wraith form sent for the purpose of sexual excitation, the succubus being the female equivalent. As has been said, when the consciousness of the witch is transferred in this way, the witch is vulnerable to the possibility of repercussion. But besides these astral projections of invoked elementals were the real monsters.

There are several recorded cases of actual vampirism, and the werewolf phenomenon was even more common. It was mentioned in the laws of King Canute and it was said that men were often turned into wolves at the change of the moon. The transformation was sometimes involuntary, and sometimes hereditary and was frequently effected by the wearing of a wolf pelt. The metamorphosis could last for three to nine years, though in some cases it only operated at nights. Werewolves could be recognized by their human eyes, though their behaviour was that of the wild wolf.

An old werewolf transformation rite could be performed by finding a fallen ash tree in the forest and reciting:

On the sea, on the island,
On the pasture gleams the moon,
On an ash tree lying,
In a greenwood, in a gloomy vale,
To the stock wanders a shaggy wolf,
Horned cattle seek his sharp white fangs,
The wolf does not enter the forest,
The wolf goes into the shadowed vale,
Moon, blunt the hunters' knives,
Break the shepherd's cudgels,
Cast wild fear upon the cattle,
On men, on all things
That they may not catch the wolf,
That they may not rend his skin.

Whilst this was chanted the operator stabbed the tree with a knife and walked around it, ending by jumping three times over the tree, whereupon he was changed into a wolf!

Of the voluntary kind of werewolf Gilles Garnier was the classic case. He was condemned to death by the court of Dôle in Lyons on 18th January 1573. He was burned alive for lycanthropy and witchcraft after more than fifty witnesses deposed that he had attacked and killed children in the fields and vineyards and devoured their raw flesh. He was sometimes seen in human shape, and sometimes as a '*loup-garou*' or werewolf. During the sixteenth century lycanthropy was particularly prevalent in France, but as wolves disappeared from England, the werewolf was replaced by the witch-hare and the witch-cat.

The wolf features largely in the old fairy tales, the story of Little Red Riding Hood originally being the story of a white-witch grandmother overcoming the power of a werewolf. In the story called "The Wolf and the Seven Little Goats" it may be noted that the wolf also 'disguises' himself.

The infamous witch-finder Matthew Hopkins swore on oath that he had seen four imps visit Elizabeth Clarke in her cell while she was awaiting trial. He described them as Jamera, a spaniel without legs, Vinegar Tom, a greyhound with the head of an ox, Sack And Sugar, a black rabbit, and Newes was a polecat. Unfortunately all of these creatures vanished after a few moments.

The familiar spirits of Alice Samuel were three in number, called Pluck, Catch, and White, but what sort of creatures they were is not made clear. The Pendle Forest witches shared a brown dog called Bull as their familiar.

It might be supposed that Matthew Hopkins was ensuring his solvency by giving such information about familiars, since he was rapidly making a fortune out of exposing alleged witches. These creatures were never exhibited in court as evidence, but the hearsay was more often than not enough to gain a conviction and execution. Since no cruelty was too great for those accused of witchcraft, the gullible or sadistic amongst the mobs would often obtain the household pets of the accused and fling them into the execution fire to be burnt alive.

Many cases of lycanthropy were the result of a form of mental derangement in which a person imagined himself to be a wolf and acted like a wild beast. As always, fact mingled with fable. For purposes of warmth as well as to create a terrifying appearance the old Norsemen wore the skins of bears or wolves they had killed, which gave rise to the word berserker, 'one wearing a bear shirt'. The expression to 'go berserk' is still with us.

Amongst primitive warriors the ascription of the savage and supernatural qualities of a bird or a beast was a commonplace. This sort of totemism has applied to every race, examples being the monkey tails and animal skins of the Zulu and the eagle feathers and porcupine quills of the Red Indians.

The remains of such beliefs can be seen today in military paraphernalia like the skins worn by drummers, and the bonnet feathers and crests of certain regiments, as well as in the animal mascots, rams, goats, horses, and dogs all being ceremonially paraded in public.

The magical protection of animals was seen in the popularity of the horned helmet, and proliferates throughout the heraldry of knighthood and families of nobility.

Another survival from Saxon times is the roof finial, the decorative tile at the top of the gable. This is the modern equivalent of the antlers with which the Saxons adorned the ends of their roofs.

Cats were such popular pets of witches that they soon became known as their attendants. After all, the precedents were numerous. The cat had been sacred in Egyptian Isis worship, and was also sacred to Frey of Norse mythology, as well as being the familiar of Diana, the witch moon goddess. It had an uncanny ability to 'see' in the dark, its eyes dilating according to the waxing and waning of the moon, and it slept in a circle, like the snake, symbolic of eternity. In short, the cat was itself an animated moon goddess. Amulets with a cat image on them were highly regarded as a protection, and to kill a cat meant seven years bad luck. Inevitably the cat became the hero of many folk tales and nursery rhymes. The cat could 'look at a king' and was a most useful familiar as Dick Whittington found out. Puss in Boots is still a pantomime hero. If a black cat came to someone's house it was lucky to keep it and take it with them if they moved elsewhere.

Before entering a new house it was customary for newly-weds to throw in a cock or a cat to appease the vengeful spirits that haunt new buildings. Cats were always useful as weather forecasters, for they could see and smell the wind, like many other animals. If a cat sneezes bad weather is on the way, just as if it sits with its back to the fire a storm is brewing. Scratching and tearing at cushions or carpets meant that the cat was raising a wind. To throw a cat overboard from a ship was to raise a fearful storm and the possibility of shipwreck. Tortoiseshell cats are lucky for their owners and hairs from their tails could be used for curing warts, though this cure was only effective if carried out in May. Sties were cured by rubbing them with three hairs from a black cat's tail on the first night of a new moon. Like the dog and the horse, the cat can see ghosts, but unlike the other two is unafraid.

Curious beliefs with regard to the dog were frequently connected with death or haunting, possibly because the animal howled in the presence of the dead. There have been many instances of a dog being so attached to its master that it literally followed him to death. If a dog howled on Christmas Eve it would go mad within the year.

In Devon it was believed that if a child died unbaptized, it became one of the Yeth Hounds which hunted the moors with the Devil. Some unredeemed sinners also turned into these demon dogs. For a living person to see the 'wild hunt' meant their premature death. Similar beliefs surrounded the Gabriel Hounds of the north country.

Equally terrifying was the barghast, a large black dog with eyes like saucers, a deity of Teutonic descent, which haunted crossroads. If it was seen by a person but not by his companion or companions, those who could not see it would shortly die unless the observer touched them, when they too would see it and be safe. The headless dog was another apparition of death.

Crossroads were frequently haunted by the spirits of suicides and those who had been executed. They were buried there because their spirits would not know which road to take when they returned after being rejected by heaven. Thus they were conveniently confined to an immediate area away from the village. Consequently crossroads were places to be avoided after dark, being so often haunted by a variety of spirits like barghasts, boggarts, headless women, and ghosts generally, as well as being frequented by those in unholy alliance such as witches, and elven folk, and by outlaws like footpads and highwaymen.

An old cure for rabies was to give the patient some of the hairs of the dog in food, giving rise to the well-known saying, 'a hair of the dog that bit me'.

Forms of good luck wishing are prevalent where the horse is concerned, even in long urbanized centres. The white horse is particularly lucky. Spells still exist all over Britain in this connection. In Scotland it is necessary to spit three times to preserve luck on seeing a white horse. In Somerset the fingers are crossed and spat over. A Welsh custom is to spit on the heel of one's shoe. In Lincolnshire the fingers should be crossed until a black dog is met with. It is unlucky to have two white horses to pull a bridal pair, but it is lucky to take a horse through the house. To have a horse with white stockings on its forelegs is fortunate, but it is unlucky to own one with a white stocking on one foreleg and one hind leg. It is unlucky to yoke or work a horse on Good Friday. On meeting a piebald one should spit and make a wish. If a horse stands with its back to the hedge a storm is coming. Horses are credited with being able to smell snakes from afar, and will not pass them. At Eckington Colliery in Derbyshire, miners were reputed to see the ghost of a white horse.

The horse was sacred from ancient times, and of the huge white horse carvings to be found in Britain, the one at Uffington in Berkshire is the oldest. Like the one at Westbury in Wiltshire it is said to commemorate Saxon victories over the Danes, but both carvings are far older than such claims would allow. It is more likely that they are tribal emblems and symbols of a religious cult. The white horse on Bratton Hill was originally a stallion with a saddle on its back and a crescent moon on its tail. Then in 1778 it was cut again to look like a conventional horse.

Below Uffington Castle is an Iron Age earthworks near a knoll called Dragon Hill, where Saint George was supposed to have slain the monster. A persistently bare patch on the knoll is where the dragon's blood gushed out and poisoned the ground so that nothing will grow there. The Uffington white horse resembles those depicted on ancient Celtic coins, having a head rather like a bird's.

The gypsies believe that a piebald horse will endow its owner with knowledge, and they preserve the secret of breeding such animals. If seeking for advice it is lucky to ask for it from the first man met who is riding a piebald, and then to follow his advice. Whooping cough in a child was cured by giving the child a ride on a piebald. Another cure for the same ailment was effected by passing the child three times over and under a donkey. An alternative cure was to eat some hairs from its back in bread and butter, and if hung round the neck in a bag, such hairs prevented fits. If the first ride of a child's life was on the back of a donkey, that child would never suffer from toothache.

These curative powers came from the cross given to the animal's back for his services to Christ on the first Palm Sunday. On the other hand, Saint Augustine related in his *De Civitate Dei* that an old woman he knew could turn men into asses by enchantments, which might invite the comment that young women have been doing the very same thing ever since. Foals are sometimes born with a sheath on the tongue which eventually falls off. If it is kept and dried, it protects its possessor from being kicked.

West country pixies were specially noted for their habit of borrowing horses at night and riding them to exhaustion so that they were unfit for work the next day. Witches were also blamed for this practice.

Here is a tonic powder for such 'hag-ridden' horses: 2 drams of sulphate of iron, 1 dram of powdered nux vomica, 2 drams of powdered carbonate of ammonia. The mixture should be given in the evening feed once or twice a week, or as required.

A secret gift known amongst the British, the Irish, and the Romanies is that of 'horse-whispering'. Various charms are whispered into the horse's ear, for different purposes. Breathing into the nostrils of the animal in a certain way is another method of charming. I have watched many a gypsy calm an enraged or frightened horse by such means.

Still in existence is an ancient and secret society usually called the Horseman's, its full title being the Brotherhood of the Horseman's Word. Initiation rites are profoundly secret and protected by solemn oaths. Membership is confined almost solely to those who make their living by the care of horses. All of the members are skilled in the knowledge of herbs concerning the diseases and cures of horses and cattle, and many are adepts in the uses of animal hypnotism. The higher initiates of this ancient society are the custodians of spells, incantations, and charms, with powers to control the wildest horse. They can irritate it or soothe it, stop it in mid-gallop, or prevent it from moving, by the use of certain words.

The clever hare or the rabbit is known to many countries and they are also regarded as familiars of Diana. The Uncle Remus stories of the American Negro slaves were akin to stories still told by African Bushmen, and animals with the cunning and adventurousness of Brer Rabbit have reached the screen of the cinema.

Women in pregnancy were once afraid to see a hare for fear of producing a child with a hare-lip, and if a hare ran across anyone's path, it was wisest for them to retrace their steps. Miners and fishermen disliked seeing a rabbit or a hare when on their way to work, and the appearance of a hare or a white rabbit in the engine-house of a pit presaged a mine accident. Yet it was lucky to carry a hare's or a rabbit's foot in the pocket. The rabbit was not to be mentioned by name at sea, just as the word 'pig' was also taboo. This resulted in rather clumsy euphemisms such as 'underground racehorses' and 'curly tails'.

As people in Lincolnshire know, a pig is best killed when the moon is waxing, and between the hours of eight and ten in the morning. And illness may be averted by walking around the pigsty three times and spitting each time. The wild boar was once sacred to Celtic and Scandinavian people, and the fear and reverence of it was transferred to the domestic pig.

The rat was another animal created by the Devil and having

a bald tail like the pig. There was however a good deal of grudging respect for an animal who was not only a cunning survivor but also one that showed courage and great parental affection. When a first tooth fell out, it was common to wrap it in paper and say, "Rat, rat, change my tooth for an iron one", a tribute to the rodent's powerful teeth. Rats also have foreknowledge, leaving houses which were about to fall down as well as deserting ships which were doomed to sink. To bring rats out of their burrows and nests, the witches used a high pitched whistle made of elderberry. This sort of rat charming is in the legend of the Pied Piper.

Mice were thought to have a connection with the souls of the dead, and it was believed that if the soul left the body during sleep it took the form of a mouse or a bee. If the soul-mouse was chased away the person would die, for his soul was lost. If a mouse ran over someone's body, that person would not live long, a belief that must certainly have often applied to witches lying in the rat and mouse infested straw of prison cells, awaiting execution. If mice invaded and overran a house where none had been before, it was a sign of a forthcoming death in the family. For a mouse to squeak by an invalid's bed, was a death portent.

It was also unlucky to meet a shrewmouse when starting on a journey. If a harvest mouse attempted to cross a path trodden by men it died at once. This belief can be partly accounted for by the frequency with which unwounded dead mice can be found on country paths and verges.

The goat was an important part of the early witchcraft rituals, or more usually a coven leader dressed as a goat in the role of the horned god. In later, Christianized times the goat was still regarded with such awe that a popular belief was current that it vanished annually for twenty-four hours, during which time he visited the Devil, to have his beard combed by his master.

Sheep were a part of the British scene ever since men turned to the pastoral life. To meet them on the road was lucky if they parted for you. The first lamb seen was lucky if facing one, but bad luck followed if the lamb had its back turned. Some said that if the lamb faced away it meant travel was forthcoming during the year. As the lamb was a symbol of innocence, it was impossible for a witch to assume its shape. To see a black lamb was doubly lucky, and a wish should be made on such an encounter. A very old belief concerned a hammer-shaped lucky bone from a sheep's head, considered to bring good fortune in the possession of sailors and fishermen. Due to its shape, the bone was known as the hammer of Thor.

If a calf had a white streak down the middle of its back it was held that it would not thrive, and for anyone to put his hand on a calf's back was to put the animal in danger of accident or death. The tip of a calf's tongue dried and carried on the person was a charm against assault and battery and also ensured a constant supply of money. The cure for contagious abortion was to bury the dead calf at the threshold of the byre so that every cow had to pass over the spot. As the carcase decayed, so the disease disappeared. There were early Christian fables about cattle too, such as the story that on Christmas Eve they knelt to adore the Saviour. Breath of the cow was sweet because she drew hay over the Holy Child and warmed Him with her breath, and for this service she was allowed a nine-month pregnancy, just like a woman with a soul.

Fairy cows were white or dun and had red ears, and were reputed to give miraculous quantities of milk. The famous dun cows of Lancashire and Warwickshire were fairy cattle, just as the white cow of Mitchell's Fold in Shropshire was a fairy cow. The equally famous Chartley cattle were white with red ears, and it was said that if ever a black calf was born from them, a member of the Ferrers family would die.

Toads were very popular familiars to medieval witches and even stones which resembled toads were valued as fortunate possessions having curative powers. Although the toad was a friend of the Devil it was lucky for a bride to see one on her way to church. In order to curse an enemy's crops a toad was set to pull a tiny plough across the field. To see a yellow frog was to anticipate good weather.

Snakes, like cats, were sacred to pagans because they symbolized eternity by sleeping in a coil. A blow from an ash stick would kill them outright, but if struck with any other wood they would linger on until the sun went down. Another protection against snakes was a raw onion, for the reptile would not come near it. It was deemed unlucky to dream of a snake or snakes, although if the dreamer got past them it signified overcoming of current enemies.

Besides using an ash stick to keep a snake at bay, another method was to draw a circle around it, make a cross sign within the circle, and then recite the first two verses of Psalm 68 which begins, "Let God arise, let His enemies be scattered".

Feathered creatures also figured largely in witch-lore, and a white cock was lucky. Cocks were supposed to crow all night on Christmas Eve to keep away evil spirits. Should a cock crow close to your door it was announcing the near arrival of visitors. If the cock crowed at midnight the angel of death was taking a soul. The heroes of Valhalla were awakened by a golden-crested cock, and the inhabitants of the underworld by a black cock, the latter bird being used for black magic all over the world.

Farmers would hang a dead duck head downwards to help get rid of evil spirits. The cuckoo was a messenger of Thor, who brought good tidings. On hearing it for the first time in the year, a wish should be made while turning some money in the pocket. It was less lucky however if the hearer was not stood on grass at the time, for the pockets would be as barren as the ground on which he stood.

If alone when a crow flew across one's path it was necessary to avoid misfortune by making the sign of the cross with the left hand, or by saying aloud, "Crow, crow, fly from my sight, or else I'll have your liver and light".

The catalogue of folk-belief concerning animals is an endless one. Corbels and other pieces of old English church sculpture perpetuate many of these beliefs. Although some churchmen like to think that the gargoyle was to scare away evil spirits, there were quite enough figures of saints to do that. The gargoyle was a spirit, the mason's artistic licence allowing him to represent astral projections or invoked demons as he imagined them to be or as they had been described in fireside tales.

At Brent Knoll in Somerset is a church with three bench-ends showing a fox dressed as an abbot. Such interpretations displayed a wry sense of humour on the part of some forgotten woodcarver.

Commonly seen in East Anglia are church fonts which have stems surrounded by carvings of wild, hairy men with clubs, perhaps showing the strength of race memory in regard to the time of the giants.

As most people could not read, the old churches were picture books for those who understood the imagery depicted in them, both biblical and pagan. Real pleasure was then derived from looking at meaningful symbolism in stone, wood, and paint. Everywhere one looked, from subsidiary carvings known as supporters to colourful rood-screens and stained-glass windows, were pictures of animals, humans, and foliage. Everything was portrayed from homely domestic life to satire and moral revelation. In the crypt of York Minster is a stone carving depicting a witch and her familiar.

At Sherborne Abbey in Dorset is a vault boss showing a mermaid complete with comb and looking glass. In the High Peak of Derbyshire there is a pool called the Mermaid's Pool. The mermaid appears on Easter Eve at midnight and she tries to allure visitors into the water. Should they not succumb to her blandishments, they are in danger of being dragged in by force. It is said that several people have thus lost their lives. On the east coast about the year 1161 some fishermen caught a tailless merman who became known as the Wild Man of Orford. He was held in the Norman castle at Orford and fed on raw flesh and fish. He was hairy, though his head was bald. Though tortured he would not or could not speak. Eventually he escaped back to the sea and was never heard of again.

Many legends and fairy tales turn the hero into a beast, with often more than a hint of the universal fertility cults. Frequently ranked against the wicked witch is the powerful fairy godmother who represents the high priestess or the mother goddess. The court jester was a descendant of the prehistoric May king, his balloon on a stick being his fool's wand.

The old fairy stories which told of men and women who understood the 'language' of bird and beast were not such nonsense after all. The faculty would have to be strongly developed, but it does exist and could be extended by training it. This was the case where a witch's familiar was concerned, and helps to some extent to explain 'sendings' or visits by birds or animals and those appearances giving premonitions of disaster. The latter were often on a different astral rate of vibrations, rather like the falling picture of poltergeist activity.

Savage people saw nothing impossible in legends that their tribes were descended from birds or beasts, or even trees. Primitive man saw animals as creatures with special gifts and obeying their own laws. Many old stories like "Beauty and the Beast" had a respect for the animal as an enchanted creature which would ultimately evolve into human shape. So many of our thoughts and sayings are coloured by their supposed wisdom, cunning, magical abilities, stupidity and so on, that it is possible to see talking animal stories like *The Wind in the Willows* and others, as being literary fossils of a time when animals took an equal place with men and were servants or messengers of hidden gods. What early man was aware of instinctively, later scientists have discovered and are discovering ever since Darwin put forward his evolution theory.

The power of control over animals and a bond between man and animal has always been the prerogative of the witch and the gypsy. Witches would often bequeath their domestic familiars to close relatives or to friends after having first taught them the care of the animals, while the gypsy hands down his knowledge in a similar way. In part this has formed the basis for the numerous fairy stories in which some animal befriends the hero or heroine, just as there are also evil spirits in animal guise.

II

BROOMSTICKS OVER BRITAIN

It was supposed that familiars had to be fed or rewarded in some way by their owners for their services. Any ordinary means of sustenance was regarded as too tame for the sensation and profit seekers to contemplate, and so it was generally alleged that the witches had little teats on various parts of their bodies with which they suckled their imps.

When the witch-finders searched the bodies of their victims for these witch marks it was not entirely due to their imaginative ideas as cruel, money-making professional torturers. Certainly any kind of natural blemish or a scar would satisfy witch-finders like Matthew Hopkins at the height of the purge.

Yet in reality, although usually unaware of the fact, they were behaving in accordance with tradition inasmuch that quite a number of witch covens practised tattooing on their initiates. Such real witch marks were rarely elaborate, being in most cases a simple round spot in red, blue, or black. The practice was an identification recalling in some respects the custom of their early British ancestors and the use of woad.

Some hereditary witches have a very small blue tattoo in woad placed below a joint of one finger and standing for a letter of the pre-Christian Celtic, or the Norse runic alphabet. Another, rather more tenuous reason for searching for supernumerary nipples may have been because several of the primitive gods had been regarded as hermaphroditic.

Totemism and belief in the magical protection of animals is a strong feeling with the British, as is evidenced by such customs as the keeping of ravens at the Tower of London. There have always been ravens at the Tower, the legend being that if they left, the edifice would fall. Six ravens are on the strength, receiving

orse-brasses handed down
om father to son protected
th owner and animal
om the evil eye.

nother method of divining
ed by witches is the
rot pack.

Gypsy matriarch.

weekly allowance of horseflesh, and being under the care of a Yeoman Warder with the title of Raven Master. In Cornwall it was held that King Arthur became a raven after death, and so the bird was never killed.

A similar legend exists concerning the Barbary apes of Gibraltar who are under the care of the army garrison. The supporters of the modern royal arms, the lion and the unicorn, have remained unchanged since 1603, and prior to that time royal animal supporters were variously the swan, the antelope, the greyhound, the bull, an imperial eagle, a boar, the white hart, and the red dragon of Wales.

In any case, the witches were frequently accused of suckling their familiars. Weight was given to this belief because it was well known that methods of maintaining animal affection can be by the use of human perspiration, hair, and even blood. There are also of course several herbal methods by which the most savage of creatures can be rendered docile.

A typical case regarding witch marks was that of Mary Sikes in 1649. She was found to have a large red lump on her side, and then a wart was found near her arm, a wart which could be pulled and stretched. At Scarborough in 1651 Anne Hunnan was given the usual search after arrest and a blue spot was found on her side. The previous year it was recorded that Margaret Morton had two black spots on her thigh, and when Katherine Earle was searched in 1654 a supernumerary nipple was found on her body. At her trial in 1664 Alice Hudson admitted that she had fed an "unclean spirit" by means of a similar tertiary nipple.

All of these kind of things were taken as clear evidence by accusers and enemies, of the suckling of imps, yet such evidence was hardly necessary since the mere accusation of witchcraft meant almost certain death.

Another common dread was that of being 'overlooked'. The practice of 'eye-biting' or casting the evil eye was credited to witches, particularly female witches. Blue or grey or green eyes were especially feared. Children were extremely susceptible to being overlooked and many charms and decorations were worn as protection against such maleficence. Coral beads or simple necklaces of red thread were worn by children, but if they happened to be without such defences the evil eye could be averted from them if an accompanying adult used a sentence with the words 'uncalled for' in it. Other alternatives were to say "the Lord be with you", or "glory be to God", or by saying, "Dear God, don't say so, protect my child", the latter to be concluded by spitting three times over the left shoulder.

A small bag of bread and salt sewn into the clothes would give protection, as would beads of alum, amber, or cowrie shells. Garlic could be carried, or the eye of a cock. In lieu of these protective measures, the evil eye could be warded off by vulgar signs such as thumbing the nose at the witch, a gesture of insolent defiance not unknown today.

To cure an overlooked child it was necessary to put a silver coin and a gold coin in water and then sprinkle the water over the child in the name of the Holy Trinity.

Being so widely used in day to day affairs the horse was also vulnerable to the evil eye. The good fortune surrounding the crescent as symbolizing the moon was always seen in the horseshoe. Any shoe cast from a horse was lucky if nailed to the door of house, byre, or stable. In Lancaster a horseshoe was fixed to the ground in one of the principal streets, having been cast by the horse of John of Gaunt.

Unfortunately the horseshoe as a lunar symbol did not protect while on the hoof, as it were. Consequently the decorative horsebrass was evolved from an original amulet designed to safeguard animal and driver from the influence of the evil eye. The crescent-shaped device was usually incorporated and such brasses were handed down from father to son. Brass was used because of its light-deflecting properties. Traditionally the positions for the various horsebrasses in Britain were on the fly-terret on the headpiece of the harness, on the brow-band, on the facepiece and the blinkers, the nose-band, the collar, the martingale, the belly-band, the breeching, the crupper, the saddle and the saddle centrepiece, and the hamepiece. This sort of arrangement belonged to the draught harness, once so beautifully displayed at shows and horse parades on May Day, Whit Monday, and so on. Many ancient examples of decorative talismans for animals have been found, some dating back to 4000 B.C. The idea of such protection was known all over the world.

It was believed that witches could foretell the future and divulge the past. There were hundreds of articles which could be used for divination and one Dutch treatise on witchcraft listed fire, air, water, earth, the dead, a sieve, a cock, an axe, a ring, ice, meal, stones, a laurel, an ass's head, smoke, a rod, pieces of wood, and rubbing of the nails.

A consecrated 'scrying stone' was much used, and the best known form of this is the crystal ball. Mirrors were also used as in the story in which the words, "mirror, mirror on the wall" are included. Actually the mirror substitute was a concave piece of glass painted black and affixed to a hollowed out wooden pedestal. The table used for the crystal ball divination should be covered by a black cloth with a triangle of white tape stitched on it, each side of the triangle being a foot long. This triangle represents the cone of power necessary to produce a form of order out of the primordial chaos of matter, the triangle symbol always being used to produce mental or physical manifestations. It is in this triangle that the crystal ball is placed. Such scrying devices should always be covered by black silk or velvet when not in use.

Some of the sybils of classical times would induce trance states by gazing steadily at a reflecting surface such as a burnished shield before they uttered their prophecies.

The crystal ball is a more modern equivalent. The oldest method involved gazing into pools of water, and some naturally formed rock basins still bear names like the Devil's Pool or the Devil's Basin or the Witches Glen and the like.

A belief in witchcraft has been implicit in all the races of mankind throughout history, and everywhere the witch was credited with the same kind of gifts. To make a clay or waxen image of an enemy has been common to ancient Babylon and to modern London. With the spells, the philtres, the charms, and knots it has perpetuated with a splendid perseverance. Substitutes for the wax or clay images were such things as sheeps' hearts, pins being stuck in them to cause illness or death, this being achieved by burying or burning the object.

The injury or fatality caused to a victim by use of a doll or effigy is sometimes attempted by a combination of sympathetic and homoeopathic magic. The sympathetic principle lies in the belief that maltreatment of the effigy results in the suffering of the person whom it represents. Homoeopathy is introduced when some part of the victim like hair or nail parings are built into the doll or mummet.

In Assyria and Babylon clay and wax figures were widely used. The names of victims were inscribed on them. Seven stalks of the date palm were then shot at them from a tiny bow. As these 'arrows' were being fired the operator said the words 'Destroyed be so-and-so', the victim being named.

This ages-old use of the doll or image is still current, though today photographs are sometimes utilized. Another version than that of personal representation is that of a figure of a hen constructed of black material and stuffed with hair of the victim, then thrown into water to rot, or it is stuck with pins and buried.

In ancient Egypt cursing was known as 'tying' and was symbolically represented by a knotted rope. Words were, and still are, most important factors in witchcraft, certain styles of utterance releasing creative or destructive vibratory forces. It is essential to accent incantations accurately to achieve the correct rhythms and hence vibrations. Witchcraft consists in getting power from the primal sources and utilizing it.

The impact of rhythmic words upon the emotions is so well known as to be often taken for granted. This impact is the stock in trade of writers and poets and composers of popular songs and advertising jingles. The 'catchy' tune will sell. People will speak of being unable to get a tune or a phrase 'out of their heads'. Staff rhymes are used or invented by children playing games, having an instinct for the rhythm which suits the case. The words may be meaningless or have irrelevancies, the poetical expression may be quite absurd and out of context, but the rhythm is accurate. The children select their staff rhymes with little regard for meaning, but a great deal for impact. When analysed the popular song may be nothing more than a revolting moan on the subject of a teenage glandular activity rendered as 'love' or more probably 'lerv'. Each form of expression has its own degree of impact, at different levels.

Every adult almost can remember some such effect from childhood whether it is "Hickory, Dickory Dock", or something similar. In a simple way this demonstrates the power of certain rhythms and sounds to be retained in the mind. Not many would care to admit it, but all human beings make up nonsense sounds of their own to express feelings. With most sophisticated people this is done either privately or only in the company of near relations. 'Bathroom crooning' is usually a personal matter.

Imagine the full power of the rhythm impact concentrated into a tremendous force and you begin to understand the incantation, the evocation, the charm, the spell, the prayer, the blessing, and the curse. The sounds we make can be uttered on the side of angels or devils, for life and hope, or for darkness and death.

Astrology was not widely practised by the early witches though a few were adepts at this form of divination. The main concern of the witch in planetary matters was with lunar symbolism.

What are now called playing cards were originally used for divination, and have been used in this way ever since. It is generally supposed that cards were brought into Europe by the gypsies somewhere about A.D. 1300 from India and Persia.

In Europe the cards evolved into the well known Tarot pack of seventy-eight cards. Fifty-six were suit cards consisting of symbols. There were swords, cups, rods, and coins. The spot cards went from one to ten, and in addition were four court cards to each suit. These suit cards were used for a minor form of fortune-telling with limited interpretations.

The remaining twenty-two cards bore symbols, pictures such as the Juggler, Hermit, Devil Fool, Strength, Moon, Lightning, and so on. These cards formed the greater arcana. It was probably in France or in Italy that the suits were changed to Clubs, Spades, Hearts, and Diamonds. This resulted in the modern playing card pack, the only survivor from the Tarot being the Joker.

The Tarot is still used in its original purpose as a symbolic alphabet of divination. In unpractised hands it is often little more than amateur fortune-telling, but in the hands of a skilled occultist can be made to reveal an extraordinary insight into personal matters.

Some witches used the Tarot, most did not. The practice was mainly confined to leading gypsy fortune-tellers.

A matter where the witches were more actively concerned was in the control of weather conditions, this being more in keeping with their traditional shamanistic role. Several methods were used. A dried liver might be burnt to raise a storm. In the East a chameleon's liver was generally used, but in the temperate zones it was that of a frog or a newt. Other operations favoured boiling a pig's bristles, or beating up water from a river, a stream, or even a puddle. Throwing sand into the air or casting flints behind the back were other means. A simple association of ideas was shown by such sympathetic elements.

Some would repeat certain words in the field of the enemy and then sacrifice a black cock at a crossroads to cause a storm of hail. Storms were also raised by stirring boiling water in which half egg shells floated.

In many ports sea witches prospered by the sale of fair winds and safe voyages. During the reign of Constantine V a man called Sopater was executed for 'binding the wind' to cause the delayed arrival of ships bound from Egypt with corn.

Every merchant sailor knows that Finns and Lapps, Shetlanders, Men of Lewis, and Manxmen often have power over winds. Threads, ropes, or even mere handkerchiefs with knots in them were sold to mariners. To loose one specific knot was to produce a moderate wind, a second knot raised a gale, and a third brought a hurricane. In the last tough days of the four-masted barques up to the 1930s many of the famous Cape Horn masters such as Captain James Learmont and Captain Ruben de Cloux were often credited with powers of 'trolling' the winds.

Scottish witches would dip a rag in water and beat a stone three times with it, saying, "I knock this rag upon this stone, / To raise the wind in the Devil's name, / It shall not lie till I please again".

To burn ferns was not only unlucky but also brought rain. Or it was enough to merely cut some ferns and then throw some flour into a spring and then stir it up with a hazel stick.

Winds should be called up at 8 a.m., 3 p.m., or 10 p.m. Beneficent winds are raised on Wednesdays when the moon is waxing. Winds for destructive purposes should be called for on Thursdays at the same hours, but when the moon is on the wane. For rain, fog, or cloud, Monday is the day if the moon is waning, while Tuesday is the time for raising electric storms. When releasing stored-up weather knots from a cord, usually red and braided in a special manner, invocations are made while turning to the east for a gale, south for thunderstorms, and west for rains. Three whistles are given for a gale, three handclaps for thunderstorms, and spitting three times is part of the operation for rain.

Through their collective power witch covens break up cloud formations to produce rain. The vibratory effects of incessant heavy gunfire on cloud masses could be well attested by any old soldier who suffered in the Flanders mud of the First World War. And yet vibrations can be produced in more silent fashion, just as the special dog whistle cannot be heard by the human ear.

There are different invocations to be used to bring conditions from zephyrs to howling gales, or mere mist to dense fog. The old device of the knotted cord or handkerchief was often sold in the days of sailing vessels, and the expression to 'raise the wind' is still commonly used. Its original meaning was that of obtaining the right wind to ensure a profitable voyage or fishing trip, in other words raising the wind meant an ultimate monetary profit. Anyone failing to raise the wind could not raise money.

Between the twelfth and eighteenth centuries it was often supposed that there was a kind of international underground society of witches. This belief was promoted by the fact that the authorities were frequently informed of mass gatherings of witches in different localities, the numbers varying according to hearsay and exaggeration.

Yet to the common people there was no need to look for witches. Everybody knew at least one person who favoured the old religion. Pagan festivals were regularly celebrated even if disguised as Christian feasts such as the 'church-ale' held in the nave of the local church, when the ordinary folk held these feasts followed by dancing at Christmas, Easter and the like. On the parapet of Cirencester Church in Gloucestershire are thirty-eight carvings representing such revellers, most of whom are playing instruments like the tabor, the rebec, and the pipe. One of the figures bears the legend "Be Merry".

What disturbed the authorities was the coven with its esbats and sabbats. The Normans, anxious to maintain their subjection of the Anglo-Saxons were always alert to the possibility of insurrection, while the Church feared a decline in the power of Christian doctrine.

The persecutors of witches unwittingly helped to propagate witchcraft. By driving the cult underground they ensured its perpetuation, for new generations are always intrigued by secrets, whereas they will often turn away from the compulsion of the over-familiar. Any powerful but persecuted minority tends to pass on its lore and knowledge and it is this inheritance which gives rise to stories of 'seventh' sons or daughters possessing strange powers.

Persecution of the witches was heightened from the fifteenth to the eighteenth century. They were hunted down by Catholic and Protestant alike, initially for the sin of heresy, additional charges being added later. During the reign of Elizabeth I there was a renewal of the campaign, returned Calvinist exiles like John Jewel, Bishop of Salisbury, being largely responsible.

But the old fertility worship proved to be remarkably tenacious. To an agricultural people the protection of crops and livestock was all important. Fertility cult deities, whether they were called Habondia, Arcadia, Cernunnos, or simply the horned god were all useful because of what they represented within the race memory. But it was imperative not to allow the conjurations to take control. They had to be servants of the will, not its master, being respected but not allowed possession. Once tolerated, possession could become permanent, leading to division of personality, to madness and death.

This was where the witch came in, as mediator and controller. Spells should only be cast when the time was propitious. The times and seasons for the working of charms was of paramount importance. Knowledge of these things was as a result of centuries of natural observation. The primary rule was that constructive, positive working should be carried out while the moon was waxing. When it was waning was the time for destructive, negative spelling. Movements of the sun, the moon, and the stars marked the power of nature in the universe, and the tides of rivers and seas indicated an ebb and flow of natural time sequences. The sun represented the masculine element of creation, while the moon was the female side of the divinity with its hidden aspects of the mind.

The four great witch festivals were Hallowe'en, 31st October, Candlemas on 2nd February. Beltane was celebrated on 30th April in England, but on 21st June in Ireland. Lammas was on 1st August. These marked each quarter of the solar cycle. The witch's year was reckoned to begin at Hallowe'en, also the beginning of the period of Nature's destruction and death. Candlemas signified the end of this reign of the lord of misrule. The vernal equinox of March which waxed until the summer solstice was indicated by Beltane, the solstice occurring about 21st June. Lammas celebrated the beginning of the period for the harvesting of fruit and crops and also signalled warning of the yearly decline back to Hallowe'en and the completion of the annual cycle to the dark winter of the death of the year.

These four major festivals were the propitious times for invoking the powers of the elements. Regulation by lunar phases provided ample opportunity to the witch to celebrate the esbat or ordinary meeting as there are thirteen full moons and thirteen new moons.

Other dates were sometimes used as sabbats such as Michaelmas, 29th September, Martinmas on 11th November, Saint Thomas's Day on 21st December, or Midsummer Eve on 23rd June. Easter time was sometimes used, the feast being moveable.

Generally speaking eight sabbats were held in a year and most witches attended a weekly esbat as well as those regulated by lunar phases. Initiation ceremonies were usually performed at one of the eight sabbats most often at Beltane or on Hallowe'en when the whole coven was present. Some covens had a matriarchal aspect, the leader being a woman variously called the lady, the maid, or the aged, even though she might be young. This high priestess could be of hereditary rank or by election. She chose a man as her high priest, an important ritualistic position. As a deputy the high priestess had another woman, who in some covens was known as the maiden. A god and a goddess were worshipped but the names by which they were known to any particular group were kept secret from the profanity of the uninitiated. Each witch was under oath to preserve such coven secrets.

To the novice they could be referred to as the horned one or the horned god, and the moon goddess or mother goddess. Initiations at one of the sabbats were not regarded as conferring any power since only constant participation in practices could bring that about. Psychic faculties had to be developed and trained.

A declaration of intent was demanded from the initiate, the coven name of the mother goddess being included in this formality. The initiate was also given a responsibility to attend esbats at least once a month at full moon, and had to give a repudiation of Christianity with the oath of loyalty to the coven. Initiation was concluded by the bestowal of a witch name upon the novice.

After other coven business had been dealt with a banquet followed, which could vary from little cakes of meal, salt, honey, and water baked with incantations to the goddess and shaped like a horned moon, to a full-blown feast. Mead, beer, or wine was drunk.

Dancing followed, consisting of a winding measure in and out to a central spot, and the witches' round, a whirling frenzy performed back to back. Dances of the follow-my-leader variety are supposed to have given rise to the expression 'devil take the hindmost'. By 1610 the witches' round was being supplanted by 'Moorish dances' or Morris dances and sabbats had in some areas become almost public affairs. The meeting dance had the leader in the middle with the rest dancing round in a widdershins direction, gradually forming a spiral towards the centre and then away again. This was, like some of the other dances, an ecstatic performance reminiscent of dervish whirling accompanied by chanting. The chain dance was based on the prehistoric hunt, the leader representing a hunted animal, the rest its pursuers. Before persecution became too intense, dances like this would wind through the villages and over the countryside.

Accompanying instruments at many sabbats were harps, lutes, pipes, and the tabor. The last instrument was the witch drum having much in common with the ceremonial drum of the ancient shaman. Painted on the surface of the small tabor was an eight-pointed star, half of which was red, half blue. These colours signified the opposites of summer and winter, male and female, birth and death, or any natural opposites. In appearance the drum was like a large tambourine, and was an article for divination as well as a musical instrument. It was used to prognosticate on recovery or otherwise from illnesses. The single skin was marked with lines forming an open octagon with a ninth line in the centre. A sigil or rune was marked over each line to give an order of direction. Nine thorn-apple seeds were placed on the drum and its side lightly tapped. The resulting position of the seeds was then interpreted.

Some of the covens called their male leader by the title of magister, or grand master. Sometimes the maiden or the lady was the daughter of the female leader. A third leader was often known as the officer, the summoner, the executor, or the man in black, his function being that of a kind of secretary and organizer. The other name of the magister might be Llew or Hugh, Cernunnos, Bok or Puck, or Robin, or even Herne if the coven was extremely traditional in outlook, this last being derived from Odin.

The queen or lady's alternative titles would be names like Nocticula, little night, Habondia, lady of love and plenty, Morrigan, Celtic goddess of death, Rhiannon, Celtic for mother goddess, or Andred, meaning witch goddess.

Names varied according to the style of the particular coven, the approach of which might be Druidic, Celtic, Saxon, or Classic. Most Druidic covens titled their leaders as master and lady, while some groups preferred Robin and Maid, in direct line with Robin Hood and Maid Marian. To complete the confusion of titles there were also covens which gave the appellation 'man in black' to their leader, or even the Devil, because of the insistence of the established Church which often declared such leaders to be nothing less.

Some of those in authority maintained that sabbats and the like were no more than the drug-induced hallucinations of a few unbalanced women, or merely drunken orgies of peasants. Others, notably the clergy, stated that the sabbats were assemblies where obscene rites took place and the Devil was invoked, to end in a riot of vile debauchery.

Actually they were to many of the peasants an occasion for enjoyment, a sort of medieval night out, when they could shout defiance at authority, feast, dance, and seek the joys of sex where possible. Unless a great many higher initiates were present ceremony was kept to a minimum.

Secrecy was advocated and emphasized from the leaders to their followers about the meeting. Some of the more loosely organized covens did not even bother to have specific days or locations for the holding of sabbats. The ordinary followers turned up in their usual clothes. It was not usual to bring the children, though this sometimes happened. During the revels there was as much, or as little, licence as the individual allowed him or herself.

In case all this seems to resemble a rugby-team coach trip, or a Saturday night pub crawl, it must be remembered that all those present held one thing in common, they were all fertility-cult worshippers. The more ordinary members were mainly expressing a temporary sense of release from the ascetic doctrines of an increasingly strict Church, a Church which they had to attempt to obey in their mundane lives, and doctrines not always adhered to by those who preached them, but who had the power to inflict penances.

But at the sabbat there was no cannibalism, no ritual murder, and no more inclination to sexual perversion than might be found in any other heterogeneous group of people. Such matters were the invention of degenerate noblemen with their private innovation of the black mass late in the seventeenth century.

The actual practice of witchcraft in the positive sense was carried out by the higher initiates of the cult at times of their own choosing and in the real coven of thirteen or so members for team working. Contrary to popular belief the baker's dozen of thirteen was not rigidly adhered to by a working coven, for this was not always possible. It was preferred because to obtain the most effective field for psychic activity where it is impossible or difficult to work individually, twelve or thirteen is usually about right. This applied to King Arthur's knights, it applies to several team sports, and to the judge and jury. There are other parallels.

Sabbats-general were special affairs for full-blown witches of more than one coven to attend. Reports from various countries of such meetings helped to give rise to the idea that there was a vast international network in operation, which was not the case.

Some favoured spots used for high coven meetings became well known to the authorities, such as the Puy de Dome in Perigord, France. Another was the Blocksburg in Germany and the Blockula in Sweden. The notorious spot in England was the Wrekin, a 1,335-foot-high hill in Shropshire. These were all suitable for restricted secret meetings, being on remote ground.

Ordinary popular local sabbats were usually held on Friday or Saturday nights after midnight. Darkness was not considered essential, and when circumstances allowed they were sometimes held at noon.

Some writers on witchcraft have inferred or concluded that coven organization presupposed the existence of a national or international leadership with a consequent hierarchy. There is no evidence of this. Groups of like-minded witches existed in different localities and knew of others or could find them. But true witches were more loosely organized than has sometimes been suggested. Like that of Romany tribes, this was their real strength, and as with Romanies there was mutual recognition, but very rarely concerted action.

People today still inadvertently use pagan methods of appeasement to the ancient gods. Belief in luck is a common example, for whenever the word is said or phrases uttered such as 'one for luck' or 'third time lucky' we are recalling Loki the mischievous god of the Norsemen.

The even more remote worshippers of the palaeolithic cults who became known as pans, satyrs, silvanuses, gnomes, goblins, elves, fairies, and by a hundred other names including witches, had affinities with legendary figures such as the Celtic Pook, Puck, or Puckle. Puck was also Robin Goodfellow, messenger of the gods and jester or clown to the fairy court. To some he was Tom Tumbler and to others a Robin Hood who in turn was identical with the German Hudkin or Hutkin, fairy king of the woods.

Although the origins of the 'merry men' were prehistoric, the Normans identified them with the Anglo-Saxons whom they had subjugated. Robin Hood's band represented a woodland coven of twelve followers and Robin himself, alternately a nuisance to the conquerors, yet helpful to friends. They wore the camouflage Lincoln green of forest fairies. They had a maid called Marian, and a useful summoner in the renegade priest Friar Tuck with his learning and knowledge of ritual. Like the Druids their meeting place was the oak tree and they were skilled with the elf-bolt or arrow.

The manifold legends which have grown up around the fairy phenomenon have resulted in some strange distortions and exaggerations, but here and there elements of truth can be discerned. Fairy rings appeared in every kind of field except the cornfield and could not be removed by the plough. They were caused by the circular dancing of witches, or fairies, which is probable at a spot where meetings were held regularly, although the common small 'fairy ring' seen today is caused by the presence of fungi. Tales were told of a blindfolded fairy, or witch, called the midwife who stood in the centre whilst the rest danced around her. The party game of blind man's buff is derived from witchcraft initiation ceremonies and practices of divination that are still in use today. Many witches were literally also village midwives, among other things, because of their medical and veterinary skills which dated from the ancient hunting and herding days. Hoods were worn, and to be hoodwinked was to be 'winked' by Hud, or to cover the eyes with the hood, an example of the English love of punning.

On the matter of witch and fairy dress, mantles of green, red, black, and in a few cases white were often worn with matching hood. The dress was not significantly different from the common dress of medieval times and can be seen today in monastic orders and academic gowns, and in the pointed hoods of the garden gnome and the nursery pixie. The colours worn held the significance of order. Green was obviously the colour of the woodland dwellers, with its own fertility symbolism. Black was favoured particularly by the male coven leaders and summoners, the 'Devils' and the 'men in black'. White was not normally a practical colour among working peasantry and so was mainly confined to special occasions for the maiden, or was the dress of the high born witch, the lady. As a symbol of purity it is seen in the pantomime and the fairy tale as the colour of the fairy godmother, the 'good' fairy, or white witch. Red and black were commonly worn as everyday dress by the village witch, giving rise to popular names such as Mother Redcap and Mother Blackcap.

Academic gowns still incorporate a colour to denote the faculty, and evocative words like greenmantle and greensleeves are still with us.

Over the centuries the fairies have been shrunk to diminutive proportions. The Brythons, the elf-people, were generally small in stature but in most other respects resembled other people. They were often nomadic, usually moving on quarter days, and so they were regarded as vanishing or appearing suddenly. Whilst in a localitv some of them would work for residents, but they often proved to be unpredictable, independent, and even eccentric servants.

Thus we get stories of the 'brownies' who brought bad luck to a house with a dirty hearth, who were fed and who worked at strange hours, so that the housework was miraculously done whilst the householder was asleep. Bread and milk would be left out for the consumption of the nocturnal visitors. Failure to leave food could mean no work being done, or at worst, wilful damage. To a kind employer, these elves were excellent, efficient workers, scuttling about as rapidly as any fairy-tale character completing some stupendous task.

Interference could however bring resentment to such independent-minded beings. At Crowle in Lincolnshire for instance there is a part of a road leading out of the town which is unfinished and will never be, because a farmer turned and watched the little men working on it, and so it was reverted to its former condition.

One of the dangers involved in visiting a fairy settlement was that time seemed different there, and what seemed like a few days could be a year, so that survivors could be aged when they returned. Not many did return, for to take food or wine there usually meant a permanent stay. The exceptions had often developed second sight. A knight who stole a fairy goblet made of horn and gold was sentenced to death for it by an Earl of Gloucester. Since it was difficult to get it returned to fairyland the goblet was given to King Henry I. Perhaps the best known fairy cup is the Luck of Eden Hall which belonged to the Musgrave family at their seat in Cumberland. The goblet is made of a greenish yellow glass and is ornamented with red, green, and blue enamelling. A metal cauldron in Frensham Church in Surrey was one that had not been returned to the fairies.

Most areas seem to have had their outposts of Brython survival at one time, but gradually as more towns were built and forests cut down the settlements of 'fairyland' disappeared. Their inhabitants died off or became dispersed amongst the ordinary population through intermarriage. The fact of absorption into the community can be seen today in the 'elfen' racial types which exist. These can be fairly easily recognized by those who are aware of the signs.

Finally to the vexed question of the witch flying on her broomstick, the belief or pretended belief incorporated into so much of the evidence given at witch-trials, and so often confessed to by the alleged witches themselves.

It has been frequently suggested that the idea of witches flying was initiated by the fact that so many Celtic peoples and others before them lived below earth level and that therefore the only means of exit was upwards out of a hole in the roof. Many of these dwellings however were inside mounds or hillocks, and so it was equally possible in such cases for an occupant to 'fly out of the window' instead of 'up the chimney'.

This explanation seems to be irrational even for an irrational age. Reports to the authorities that a witch had been seen going through the roof or out of the side of a hill might be construed as meaning that they flew, but it presupposes that the authorities were not only excessively naïve, but that they were also unaware of the types of dwelling houses in their own country. Even granting that the authorities in any age are suspected of being notoriously ignorant of what really goes on amongst the ordinary people, this could hardly have been the case here.

How many people I wonder, have concluded a brief conversation with the remark, 'I really must fly'? How often have people been reported as having been seen 'flying down the street'? Finally, how many witches or alleged witches have made such remarks themselves, to have them seized upon as yet more evidence of their satanic powers.

Isobel Gowdie said in one of her confessions that she had a pony which could fly as the straws could fly along the highway. Capital could be made out of such an innocuous remark by avid sensation seekers.

Another view strongly held, perhaps with more justification than the hole in the roof theory, is that witch flying was a hallucination induced by drugs.

Certainly several confessions included references to a 'flying' ointment. Here are two of the recipes used by some witches on occasion. Aconite boiled with poplar leaves and parsley, and mixed with fat and soot, to make an ointment base. Aconite contains the deadly poison aconitine. The root of the plant contains about four per cent alkaloid and one fifteenth of a grain of such alkaloid is lethal. Monkshood is a popular name for a variety of aconite. Rubbed on the skin, the aconite in the ointment would produce a tingling sensation followed by numbness of the area. Fumes from the other ingredients would also combine to produce the overall effects of light-headedness and hallucination.

Another preparation contained aconite with hemlock and belladonna. Hemlock contains another alkaloid poison called conine, while belladonna is the deadly nightshade from which atropine is extracted. This mixture would also give hallucinations and in some cases impressions of flying or leaping through the air, like putting on the mythical seven-league boots.

Other factors contributing to the belief in witch flying, along with self-interested reports of witch-finders, were the general beliefs in flying myths and allegories. The Valkyries of the Norsemen flew, and so did the Christian angels. Indeed the early English spoke of creatures called *waelcyryean* who were identified with witches. So to the populace at large it might have been thrilling to hear that convicted witches had flown, but not all that much of a surprise to people raised on fireside stories of weird happenings and miracles.

Yet another explanation is that witches dreamed of flying, or that it was a matter of astral projection. The last suggestion is an extremely valid one, since astral projection is a feature of true witchcraft.

A further possibility is that of levitation, not unknown to the ecstatically devout, pagan or otherwise. There is however no evidence for this in records of old-time witchcraft. Some of the stories of being in fairyland for years and then returning could also be variations on the theme of astrally-projected absences, also giving rise to tales such as that of Sleeping Beauty, and much later, Rip Van Winkle.

Concerning the tradition of the broomstick, the staff or sign of benediction has long been that of the cross. It has variations ranging from the ancient Indian and Tibetan swastika, the trident of Neptune, the magical Excalibur sword, the hammer of Thor, the magic wand and the broomstick, to the crozier in the hand of the Christian bishop.

The pitchfork and the drover's stick was the badge, the staff of the yokel, while the broomstick was the female equivalent, being both a phallic and a domestic symbol. The true medieval broomstick had an ash handle for strength, birch twig or broom bristles, birch being one of the ancient sacred trees, and the whole was bound with willow, the tree most sacred to Diana the moon goddess. Herdsman used an ash stick to keep evil away from the cattle they drove.

The Norsemen and the early mythology of Greece maintained that the ash tree was an ancestor of man. Norse gods created the first man called Askr out of this tree, so the magical connotations are obvious. Some witches made their mommets or dolls out of ash wood to practise effigy spells.

As a defensive weapon then, the ash was much carried. The broomstick was so closely associated with women that even today a woman is sometimes referred to as an old besom, and the walking stick is descended from the pilgrim's staff and the crook and pitchfork. In 1945 an unsolved ritual murder was committed in England, the weapon used being a pitchfork. Peasants who lived in marshy districts like the Lincolnshire fens often used walking boards and stilts to cross watery stretches, a circumstance which gave rise to a subsidiary rumour that witches could also walk on water.

Accusations levelled at witches were always more welcome if they included supernatural marvels. It suited the authorities to exemplify such cases as breaking the laws of God, and it gave entertainment to an unlettered people, temporary relief from consideration of the harsh circumstances of their own lives.

So the maligned witch could not simply fly off to her coven meeting taking her broomstick with her, she must literally fly on it.

12

THE WICCAN

The accusations levelled at the wiccan, the witches of old times, were those of venefic magic, natural magic, casting of spells, storm-raising, shape-changing, and the keeping of familiars. Some of the modern equivalents are weather forecasting, faith healing, and dealing in herbal remedies.

By the seventeenth century, some 200 years of persecution had taken toll and most of the organized centres of witchcraft had been destroyed, the members burnt, hanged, or tortured to death. The survivors had scattered and gone underground. Throughout the ages the wiccan, the wise ones in the old English tongue, retained the memory of their ancient religion and saw to its continuance, albeit in secret. But who were these witches and what were they like?

In the home it was the wife who mostly preserved the charms and curses handed down by ancestors. She was traditionally the depository of medical lore and was regarded as the source of life and fertility, a guardian priestess of the race with mysterious power over childbirth, and therefore by extension, over crops. Thus she had wisdom and magical knowledge vested in her.

When social control shifted almost wholly to the man she lost her high place. Aspects of Christian doctrine helped her downfall, particularly that aspect which suggested that through her sin came into the world.

The tribal priestess of paganism became the hated witch in Christian belief, but yet the tradition of secret power and knowledge continued. Woman's care of children had resulted in a knowledge of medicines, of experimentation with foods best for nourishment, and the discovery of foods which were less beneficial. She had learned by experience and by inheritance the values of simple potions and cures. She had learned, some better than others, how, when, and why such medicines and cures should be administered or applied.

Women had been able to relieve many of the pains of mankind, but the reverse aspect of this power was the ability to work harm. As always, woman could be as seductive as Circe, or as haglike as Hecate.

The witches of Macbeth actually existed. They were not sisters and they lived near Glamis and were consulted on Hardmoor Heath. A famous Scottish male witch was Coinneach or Kenneth Odhar Fiossaiche, known as the Brahan Seer. He was born on the island of Lewis about 300 years ago and like Mother Shipton he was renowned for his gift of prophecy, foretelling the coming of railways, which he described as "long strings of carriages without horses". In other prophecies he detailed the coming of piped water and gas, the Caledonian Canal, and the battle of Culloden. His predictions were made with the aid of a blue stone which a spirit had told his mother she would find in a lake and that she must give to her son. At her own insistence he told the Countess of Seaforth that her husband was having an affair with a woman in Paris. Far from being grateful for this revelation, the Countess had the Brahan Seer executed for witchcraft, but before his death he forecast the future of the House of Seaforth to its fall.

As an illustration of the kind of powers which can be harnessed by ordinary people, but of which many of the witches have knowledge, there is the remarkable example of a Frenchman called Bottineau. He was a beacon keeper on the Indian Ocean island of Mauritius in 1764. Purely by natural observation he discovered that he could forecast the arrival of ships to the island up to a week before they appeared over the horizon. From 1778 until 1782 he announced in advance no fewer than 575 ships, none of which arrived until at least four days after they could possibly have been seen by the human eye. Bottineau's claims were regularly and officially tested by the Governor of Mauritius, always being found to be accurate. Bottineau called his method 'Nauscopie' and explained that he could see in advance a kind of vacuum in the air which always preceded vessels long before their appearance.

This was natural divination, although Bottineau was not a witch.

In the broadsheets and pamphlets of England there emerged a standardized image of the witch that is still with us in books and films of today. A composite standard picture had been formed of a cloaked, steeple-hatted old crone hurtling through the air on a broomstick or sitting by the fire with a cat familiar, presumably directing evil thoughts at her neighbours. She was invariably ugly and old, with hooked nose and jutting chin, and was never seen without her hat.

The perfect model for this kind of witch was the famous Mother Redcap, also known as Mother Damnable or the Shrew of Kentish Town. She was the daughter of Jacob Bingham, a brickmaker by trade who had been in the army and who had married a pedlar's daughter while he was in Scotland.

When Jacob left the army he resumed his old trade in Kentish Town, combining it with occasional travels as a pedlar, on which jaunts he was accompanied by the family.

Jinney, as the daughter was called, had a child by a gypsy called George Coulter when she was sixteen. They lived together but unfortunately Coulter was hanged at Tyburn for sheep stealing. After that, Jinney took up with a drunkard called Darby who caused her much trouble. Then Darby went missing, and Jinney's parents were arrested and hanged for witchcraft.

Next Jinney lived with a man called Pitcher. Eventually the body of this man was found in the large oven, where he had burnt to death. Jinney was then tried for his murder but was acquitted because it was known that Pitcher had a habit of hiding in the oven to escape from her harsh tongue.

Thereafter Jinney, or Mother Redcap as she had become known, lived alone for some time. She was rarely seen except at night in the lanes of the area. People feared her and could not understand how she existed. Then one night during the Commonwealth troubles a stranger, apparently pursued by enemies, turned up at her cottage, and her home became his sanctuary for several years until he died. During that time the sounds of blows and arguments were heard by passers-by.

It was popularly believed that Mother Redcap had poisoned the unidentified man, but though an inquest was held, no proof was forthcoming. She lived on in the cottage her father had built on waste land, hated and feared and never seeming to want for money, and prepared to use her foul tongue against anybody, and sometimes being baited in return. Any local mishap was blamed upon her, but she continued to look sullenly out of the half-door of her cottage at people who passed.

Little mobs who gathered to jeer at her would retreat hastily when they saw her black cat jump on to her shoulder. Yet people did consult her as a witch, for fortune telling and for cures for their ailments.

Mother Redcap was found one day, where she had died by the fireplace, seated and surrounded by pots of herbs. A public house was eventually built on the site of her cottage. It was named the Mother Redcap, and became a feature of modern Camden Town.

In Mother Redcap we have a picture of the traditional storybook witch, a hook-nosed old crone wearing a cloak and a grotesque red hat, peering from the hatch door of her cottage, black cat by her shoulder.

The lonely old woman living in a hovel with an animal for company, and seen collecting herbs in the countryside by day or night became the popular conception of the witch. If her secret cures worked she could be tolerated, if they failed then harsh punishment might be her lot. Many other types of persons were accused of witchcraft including children like the two boys hanged and burnt at Paisley in 1697, but it was the cloaked figures of the Mother Redcaps that became synonymous with the word witch.

As we have previously seen, the earliest phase of witchcraft was that of the witch-doctor, the shaman whose authority was greater than that of any other member of the tribe including the chief. A second phase followed when the status of the witch-doctor became that of an intermediary between gods and men. This was eventually superseded by the idea of a semi-divine royalty, an extension of the role of witch-doctor, so that a priestly class was led by an all-powerful ruler.

Alongside this grander aristocratic scheme there always flourished the local witches. These were the regional 'cunning men' and 'cunning women' who worked at a social and geographical distance from the centres of national power, and they were a necessity when doctors were few and available only to the rich. Such custodians of health-giving secrets were persons of importance to a community, occasionally loved, sometimes feared, but always respected.

People travelled miles to Zennor in Cornwall to have themselves or their children charmed for 'wildfires', which was another name for *erysipelas*. They went too for tooth pains, for rheumatic ailments, and for 'kennels' or eye ulcerations. The charmers were both men and women, who maintained that their secrets could only be passed on to a member of the opposite sex.

In medieval days disease was rampant, the predominant cause being hunger, resulting in poverty of the blood and the emaciaation so often seen in the sculpture of those times. When blood was almost as thin as water, scrofulous complaints were all but universal.

Only the very rich could afford the cost of hiring the services of the few Arab or Jewish physicians available in Europe. During periods when disease was particularly virulent the poor could only crowd at church doors waiting for blessings and aspersion by holy water. In droves came the sick, pleading for help, only to be told that God was afflicting them as sinners but that they should be thankful since their suffering would be that much less in the life to come, and the Church would pray for the dead.

Consequently the people turned increasingly back to the witches for the relief of their bodily ills, if not for spiritual salvation, and if these men and women were so cunning in the cure of skin eruptions, then it must follow that they were equally wise in other matters. And so the wise men and women, the cunning white witches, the guisers and blessers, were credited with many powers.

Following on the appearance of the Black Death about 1348 there came the scourge of Saint Guy's or Saint Vitus's Dance. This form of *chorea* allied with other contributory diseases caused people to fall into epileptic convulsions, affecting hundreds as if by transmission, people grasping hands and whirling until they dropped dead from starvation or heart exhaustion. Spectators would sometimes roar with laughter until they themselves felt compelled to join in the dance of death.

Had this wave of disease and insanity not been arrested the phenomenon might have continued to spread until the whole of Europe had become demented. Witches were present at the centre of activity administering their herbal remedies, their *Solanaceae* or 'herbs of consolation', remedial measures for the classes of disease encountered.

The great Paracelsus claimed that he learned most of what he knew as a physician from wise women, sorcerers, shepherds, and hangmen. Executioners were notoriously clever at bone-setting. The witches made great use of herbs, of which they had an unrivalled knowledge. They used calmants and stimulants which by long experience had proved to be of advantage to their patients.

Yet it was extremely dangerous to employ some of these herbs, and dosages were determined often by the audacity of the practitioners, some of whom displayed a genius as healers. The witches ran fearful risks for few laymen at that time appreciated that certain poisons applied internally or externally in small doses acted as remedies.

Found in a woman's possession, some of the witch herbs could lead to her being accused as a poisoner or an agent for the concoction of evil spells. She might then be stoned to death by an angry mob, or made to undergo trial by water or being weighed against the parish Bible, or be dragged off to the church where the clergy could make a pious ritual of her ultimate death at the stake, an edifying spectacle for the people watching the consuming flames, and a warning against straying from righteousness.

Even though occasionally knowledgeable monks were hired to eliminate enemies of the Church by poisoning, in general that establishment had a genuine horror of poisons. It was felt that only forces of the Devil could utilize them as remedies. And where priestly benedictions apparently failed, the witches could provide their clients with ease, virility, forgetfulness, love, and so on, and some of them could even bring relief by the use of magnetic passes. Clearly this was an opposition which could not be lightly tolerated by authority.

Then when linen became widely used as a substitute for wool, many skin diseases such as leprosy lost much of their virulence, though the connection was not generally recognized at the time.

At their sabbats the witches would infuse their herbs in beer or cider or hydromel. Hydromel was a drink made from honey and water somewhat resembling mead, while cider was a relatively new beverage introduced in the twelfth century.

But much more was expected of the cunning men and women besides the ability to heal. They were frequently consulted. The witch women were often the village midwives and both male and female witch acted as marriage counsellors, general psychologists, as well as hypnotists and local detectives. They were skilled at finding the bodies of drowned persons, often using clothing of the deceased which would float over the spot where the corpse lay. Two other methods used were the firing of gunpowder over the river to cause the body to rise to the surface, and the floating of a loaf of bread containing a little mercury, which stopped over the place where the drowned person was hidden, two methods which are detailed in Mark Twain's novel *Huckleberry Finn.*

The white witch also had to act as an antidote to the black witch, curing people and cattle who had been cursed, and remedying all manner of evil spells like 'ill-wishing' and 'overlooking'. Methods of irrigation, knowledge of underground springs, of water-divining, were also expected of the wise man or woman.

Witches could send murrains on cattle, or remove them, and the modern veterinary surgeon can do the same. Stories of fabulous horses that were unbeatable in races or trials of strength were related in the shires, but today there would have to be a 'dope test'.

Witches were also supposed to be able to induce or prevent childbirth, blight crops or improve them, part or unite lovers, raise storms, cause lingering illnesses and death by image-making. Their children sometimes inherited their powers since they were usually dedicated to the witch god by their parents, or as some thought, to the Devil.

Within these functions of divining for lost property, discovery of thieves and other miscreants, healing and dispelling of maleficent curses were black, grey, and white witches. Black witches were avowed enemies of good, while the grey witch was an unknown quantity capable of good or bad activities but usually neutral unless crossed, whereas the white witch was the good fairy godmother. They might therefore be compared to the three fates, Atropos who cut the thread of life, Lachesis who measured its length, and Clotho who spun its thread.

A spell was usually an incantation or a written instruction for harmful influence, and a charm was for the opposite purpose. Even now, in the case of a dubious relationship or an apparently baleful influence at work, we are apt to make remarks like 'he seems to be under a spell', whereas the successful conclusion to some affair 'worked like a charm', or we may know someone who leads 'a charmed life'.

A talisman was a form of portable psychic power and could be almost anything that had been charged or 'blessed' by a witch, made for a specific purpose, often with a spell inscribed on it, an Aladdin's lamp. An amulet was an object having a beneficial effect upon its owner.

The spells used in the Middle Ages were often macaronic, a mixture of two or more languages, usually English and ill-used Latin, adopted because of the assumed power of the new Christian religion.

Used in conjunction with binding with split reeds, this charm was often used for dislocated joints: "Motas, danata, daries, dardaries, astataries". A popular toothache charm was to repeat: "Galbes, galbat, galdes, galdat". An alternative was to write on a paper to be used as an amulet these words: "Strigiles, falcesque, dentatae, dentium, dolorum persanate". Rabid dog bites required "Irioni, khiriori, effera, kuder, fere", written on a piece of bread and swallowed, or "Hax, pax, max, Deus adimax" could be inscribed on an apple which was then eaten.

Fevers could be combated by washing the hands with the patient and reciting Psalm 144, or holding the patient's hand and saying,

"Acque facilis tibi febris haec fit, atque Mariae Virgini Christi partus".

For epilepsy the following was considered useful: "Gaspare fert myrrham, thus Melichior, Balthasar aurum Haec tria cui secum portabit nomina regum Soluitur a morbo Christi pietate caduco". An alternative to this was to take the hand of the sufferer and say in his ear: "I conjure you by the Sun, the Moon, the Gospel of the Day, given of God to Saint Hubert, Gilles, Corneille and Jain, that you get up without falling again, in the name of the Father, Son, and Holy Ghost, Amen". This charm showed a mixture of incorporated beliefs in both Basque witch gods and in Christianity.

Two spoken charms for staunching bleeding were: "In nomine Patris et Fili et Spiritus Sancti, carat, cara, sarite, confirma consana imabolite", or "Sepa, sepaga, Blood cease to flow. All is consummated in the Name of the Father, podendi, and of the Son, pandera, and of the Holy Spirit, pandorica, peace be with you, Amen".

Obviously such charms show a degree of literacy and owe much to early Christian ritual. But they also displayed a heterogeneous mixture of beliefs and languages. Along with the dog-Latin and the English were bits of the secret witch tongue based on old Basque words. Jain or Jainco was sometimes evoked along with orthodox Christian figures, and the expression 'By Jingo', known to the twentieth century is a corrupt form of an oath to the old witch deity in much the same way as the swear word 'bloody' is a corruption of an early Christian expression, 'By Our Lady'.

The theft of consecrated wafers for magical use showed a healthy respect for some aspects of Christian power, as did the stealing of holy water. Wafers were sometimes used in love philtres among other things. Holy font water could be used for baptizing dolls for death spells or for healing purposes, and from the thirteenth century bishops began having church fonts covered and locked, as many still are today.

A cure for shingles was to take a needle and thread and to make as if sewing into the shingles while actually sewing the air around them. The recital to this was: "I pierce this rash with this needle. Out rash. I see you whole, I see you well and happy as I stitch away your pain." Then an ointment of mutton fat and dust was made and applied once a day for nine days.

On seeing a ghost it should be addressed thus: "In the name of the Lord, why do you visit me?" The ghost would then explain the reason for the visitation. A less friendly approach was: "I command you in the name of God and his angels, speak!" Having then replied by explaining its trouble, and the reason for its presence, the ghost would expect the listener to attempt to remedy the matter at the earliest opportunity. The point was that a ghost could not speak unless it was first addressed.

To prevent the recurrence of nightmares the word 'slad' should be repeated in the mind before going to sleep. The word 'krub' should be repeated to ensure against sleeplessness. To stop worrying the word 'blare' should be repeated, while depression could be cured by the word 'weel', while to repeat 'aberdan' was to promote virility.

A man could impress a woman if he first repeated to himself, "Nades, suradis, Maniner". To declare "Ritas, Ambas, Zamareth" prior to study or an exam or interview was to ensure favourable results. Luck in a card game would come if 'Pilates' was pronounced while shuffling the pack. To hit a lucky number in other games of chance 'Rokes' was the required word.

One way of removing the spell from an overlooked person was to take a silver coin as big as a sixpence while the victim was seated before a good fire, and lifting as much salt as the coin would carry place the salt in a tablespoonful of water. The mixture was then stirred gently with the forefinger until the salt was dissolved. Then the soles of the victim's feet and the palms of his hands were rubbed or bathed with the solution. Finally the wet finger was drawn across his forehead, then the operator flung the remaining contents of the spoon into the fire saying, "God preserve from all harm", or else "Preserve from the eye of the Devil". This should be done in private without any interruption, and no other words should be spoken during the operation.

Many of the old spoken charms and spells had a dash of Latin or something from the English Bible to convince the religious Christian, and this of course gave rise often to charges of blasphemy. Saint Appolonia was frequently invoked against toothache, Saint Columkill against fire, Saint Gabriel for gout, Saint Blaise for bone troubles, and Saint Job for animal diseases, particularly in sheep.

There were few professional healers other than the witches and one group which proved exceptional was the famous Myddrai physicians. These Welsh wizards with overtones of Druidism were supposed to have derived their knowledge from a fairy called the Lady of Llyn y Van Vach. The physicians compiled a book containing about a thousand simples in the thirteenth century.

Despite almost universal illiteracy, witchcraft practices were recorded in books from time to time. Some of the earliest known magical books were those of the Chaldeans. One of them, *The Wicked Spirit*, was filled with conjurations and imprecations, formulae designed to repulse demons, to avert their actions and preserve the invoker from attack. A second book contained incantations having the power of curing various ailments. The third book of the series had in it hymns to certain gods. Supernatural power was attributed to these chants.

The *Book of Thoth* was an ancient Egyptian book containing secret lore of the magician priests of the Nile valley.

Scottish witches had a grimoire or magical book called *The Red Book of Appin*. The word 'grimoire' for books of occult lore seems to have become popular, but in the old days the word 'gramary' was in use for the English books. This is practically the same as the word grammar and is correct. In my possession is a tape recording of an old American lady singing a traditional song concerning teaching the children the 'gramary' meaning occult lore. The recording was made in the hilly backwoods of West Virginia and is an interesting example of transportation of witchcraft by early settlers, and of its survival.

Another grimoire, still in use in America, is called *The Long Lost Friend*. It was a New England importation but was also popular in Pennsylvania and other nearby states.

People who had worshipped at sacred groves and wells were pressured into conformity, and during this attempt at stamping out paganism monastic authorities often preserved in writing or in symbols those practices to which they were opposed. In this manner several grimoires were preserved for posterity. Through this a good deal of occult tradition has emerged from Christian monasteries, several of which had comprehensive treatises on witchcraft and magic.

One ancient grimoire is entitled *The Goetia*, being a book devoted to goety or black magic. It contains instructions for the invocation of negative, destructive forces, seduction by use of potions, and prophecy by necromancy. There was also a similar grimoire known as *The Black Book*.

The tradition of witchcraft was mainly oral and the major recognizable 'official' book of the cult was, and is, The Book of Shadows. This is not a formally printed work and ideally is copied in the witch's own hand, to be destroyed at death, or in the times of persecution when danger threatened. It was boldly written because it might have to be consulted by firelight, candlelight, or even moonlight. It never left its owner's possession. Generally the book was the property of one member of a coven, the summoner or magister or other high initiate. Some covens kept a space in the book in which to record the names of the members, though for obvious reasons of security these were their witch titles, not their real names. It also contained herbal lore, a brief history of the craft and details of secret rites and descriptions of spells and their working. It was often expected that the contents of the book should be committed to memory in case it had to be destroyed.

All primitive peoples preserve and perpetuate their histories through memories and legends of their elders and in songs, dances, rhymes, and proverbs. Lack of literacy does not mean lack of intelligence, and the story-tellers among such people as the Romanies are the living books of the community. Each generation is linked to its predecessor by verbal advice, allegory, or myth. True witchcraft was a lore handed down from generation to generation by the firesides of peasant cottages. Immeasurably old, it belonged to the history of the race itself.

Several of the names of the most famous of the cunning men and women are still remembered today within the Craft, such as Timothy Crowther, a white witch of about 1730, the white witch

Bridget Bostock of Nantwich in the 1780s, Isaac Rushworth the cunning man of Leeds around 1857, James Tunnicliffe of the same time, in Derby, and the cunning man Murrell still remembered in Essex from the 1850s.

The cunning men were diviners, popular healers, discreet in their activities. Their patients and clients were mostly from the peasant and artisan class, and consequently not much has been written about them. One classic exception to this was John Harries who was born in Carmarthenshire in 1785. He studied medicine in London but without gaining a qualification. Then he began in practice as a cunning man. Before long he had clients coming to see him from far away. He practised astrology and used a mirror for scrying and always maintained that he derived most of his knowledge from the world of spirits. Once a year he went to a remote spot and recited the appropriate conjurations within a magic circle to renew his supernormal powers for another year.

He forecast the day of his own death, which occurred in 1839 when he slipped from a ladder and broke his neck, while helping to fight a fire. His tombstone in Caio churchyard reads, "John Harries, Surgeon". The practice was taken over by his son who continued in the activities of a local cunning man, or '*Dyn hysbys*' in Welsh.

ⱃoof finials like
nese derive from
ne Saxon
ustom of
lacing antlers
t the ends of
oofs.

Lincolnshire
itch well.

Rather than a defence against evil spirits, the gargoyle was the stone mason's creation of a spirit, perhaps by astral projection.

13

PHARMACOPOEIA

The word pharmacopoeia is from the ancient Greek, and its original meaning was not only the compounding and use of drugs, but also the casting of spells and charms, in other words, witchcraft.

Many of the 'cures' the white witch was expected to obtain were those against ill-wishing or curses put upon people by other witches. Defences against such black-witch power were absorbents like vinegar, sliced onion, and garlic. Iron too was useful since in specific forms it had a 'scrambling' effect, rather like static interference in radio-wave reception.

A peeled, cut onion in the bedroom prevented colds, and was useful when rubbed on wasp stings. Raw onion was also carried in the pocket as a rheumatism preventative. Onions boiled in molasses were given in cases of sore throat. Where throat ulcers were present, benefit was derived from inhaling the vapour of hot vinegar. To give an instant hiccough cure brown sugar was moistened with vinegar, a few grains being taken to a teaspoonful of vinegar.

I was once told by a witch from Zaire how to cure malaria by placing sliced onions around the feet, binding them in as close a manner as possible. The onions would then draw away the fever. This is on the same principle as that of strewing garlic about a room to draw off evil effects. Garlic used overnight should then be burnt. Onions were sometimes called witches' apples and were used in many anti-evil charms.

The witch fraternity in all ages have possessed a remarkable knowledge of drugs, potions, unguents, and herbs generally. They knew of the poppy which gave sleep and dreams, of hemp which gave visions, datura which induced a loss of memory, of blighted grains which upset life cycles, barks that killed love, and insects which aroused desire.

In favour at some witches' sabbats in Europe was bufotenin obtained from the skins of toads, and they also used scopolamine, henbane, belladonna, and harmine, an alkaloid from seeds of wild rue, and similar to the drug yage which comes from a vine of the Amazon Basin. Another very toxic alkaloid was the fly-agaric, a hallucinogenic being obtained from this British fungus, and once used by some Viking berserkers and by ancient shamans to achieve trance states.

Although regarded by some as hocus-pocus, witchcraft has produced a great deal of genuinely useful medical discovery. In the eighteenth century a certain Doctor Withering observed that a wise woman was able to cure the dropsy with one of her herbal remedies. He bought the recipe from her and found that its major ingredient was foxglove. From this came the knowledge of the drug digitalis now also used in certain forms of heart disease, and one of the most valuable drugs known to medical science. As well as the alkaloid, the leaves of the foxglove also yield up several poisonous glucosides. From this discovery Doctor Withering gained great fame, but of the obscure Shropshire witch from whom he obtained the recipe there is no record.

Usually herbs should be gathered when in full flower and during the waxing of the moon or when the planet governing a particular herb is rising. Leaves should be gathered when fully grown. Herbs should be dried in the sun if possible and then kept in paper bags so as to keep their colour and smell as long as possible, for often when they have lost colour and odour they are no longer useful.

The planets ruling various herbs are considered important in real witchcraft herbalism, but not everyone has sufficient astrological knowledge to abide by such rules.

As an example of planetary influences the following may be of interest. Agrimony comes under Jupiter and is good for heart, liver, chicken-pox, diarrhoea, and scarlet fever. Herb bennet or avens is also under Jupiter and is good for the liver and blood and provides a general tonic and antiseptic. Dandelions similarly are good for liver and blood. Dock is also governed by Jupiter. There are different varieties such as bitter, fiddle, sorrel, and yellow. But the water dock is best, its powdered root treating ulcers and rickets. The Witches' Tree, the elder, comes under Jupiter. There is no part of it that is not used in folk medicine for some purpose, and it is specially useful for fevers and rheumatism.

Not to be confused with it is the alder, under Venus, good for rheumatism and aching feet, a decoction of hot leaves being placed on the affected area. Burdock is used for rheumatism and gout, and ground ivy or alehoof is for treatment of spleen, stomach, and lungs. Boiled with a little honey, the juice is good for sores and ulcers. Still under Venus, mint makes a good tea for stomach upsets, while groundsel is used in cases of colic and jaundice.

Mercury governs horehound, a tonic for general use and against coughs, while marjoram will relieve convulsions and cramps. Saturn rules ivy, which can be used for certain skin complaints. The nettle comes under Mars, a good blood tonic, used for arthritis, and also in cases of nose bleeding. Ruling coltsfoot or coughwort is the Sun and like rue it has heart-strengthening properties, while the bruised leaves are helpful in cases of sciatica. Coltsfoot is also a cure for coughs.

Arum, known also as cuckoo pint, comes under the Moon. It has poisonous leaves and berries. The root is used for gout and rheumatism, and it is best preserved in dry sand. Romanies treat boils with the leaves and are the only herbalists who use other than the root.

When planting herbs, those from which only the root will be required should be planted while the moon is waning. Those intended for use of flowers or leaves should be set during the moon's waxing.

For those who would like to divine with a crystal ball it might be noted that juice of the mugwort applied to it is supposed to impart strength to its prophetic property. This herb is one of the *artemisia*, under lunar influence. Artemis, after whom the plants were named, was a Greek title for Diana the moon goddess.

The foregoing is obviously not an exhaustive list, since this is not a treatise on herbalism, and it is as well to warn readers that it is extremely dangerous to play about with certain herbs unless they know what they are doing or are acting under expert guidance.

For instance the fly-agaric toadstool is so called because it was often used mixed with milk for killing flies. Doses of such fungi quickly produced delirium, madness and death in human beings.

Deadly nightshade or belladonna, known also sometimes as dwale, is the most poisonous plant known to botany, containing several alkaloids, mainly hyoscamine, atropine, and hyoscine. Its poison can be absorbed through the skin and it should be left strictly alone. Fashionable women once used extracts from it to enlarge the pupils of their eyes, hence the Italian name Belladonna or beautiful lady.

Second only in deadliness to belladonna is henbane, well named as being dangerous to hens as well as to other birds and animals and human beings.

Another vicious plant is the thorn apple, having similar properties as those of belladonna and henbane. In the U.S.A. it is sometimes called jimson weed. It is used by experts in the treatment of asthma, the extract being stramonium.

This poisonous family of plants includes the tomato and the potato. Potato leaves are similar to those of Deadly Nightshade, atropine and solanine being found in them, but the tubers are perfectly safe when cooked.

All members of the *Solanaceae* family are more or less poisonous because they contain varying amounts of alkaloids and poisonous glucosides. Hyoscine in association with morphia is used medically as an analgesic.

Lettuce contains small amounts of hyoscyamine, which is why it is regarded as a soporific. The highly poisonous berries of the cuckoo pint cause blistering and swelling of the tongue if eaten. A scarlet thistle, *Carduus heterophyllus*, was popularly known as the melancholy thistle, because a decoction of it taken in wine would expel melancholy.

Hemlock, as is well known, is yet another extremely poisonous plant containing conine and coniccine, bitter alkaloids which cause vomiting, severe colic, delirium, and increasing paralysis to death.

But equal parts of herb grace and sage, about three or four leaves of each put into a glass of beer and drunk twice a day, morning and night, is good for arthritis.

A flower called hound's tongue was supposed to stop dogs from barking. Leaves were placed underneath the feet and thereby the dogs were silent in the presence of that person. This might sound like an old wives' tale, but certainly if the leaves are crushed and made into a potion they can produce lassitude or even paralysis.

Perhaps the most curious ingredient of the witches' pharmacy was the white bryony or *Bryonia dioica*, otherwise known as the mandrake. It was taken just after a new moon, being found in hedgerows or on wasteland, the best time being between the winter solstice and the vernal equinox. The taking had to be done unobserved and a deosil circle was drawn around the plant, using the athame, the witches' ritual and working black-handled knife. The plant had to be dug up without it being damaged, and it is usually necessary to tug hard to extract it, which was when it was said a groan could be heard.

Next the foliage was trimmed off the main stem, a small piece of root being left and replanted in the same spot. The main portion of root was then carved in the features of a little person of the opposite sex, again using the athame and repeating, "Guard this home in the name of Hertha". It was then placed in a churchyard or else planted at a crossroads after another deosil circle had been drawn. For twenty-eight days after its original uprooting it had to be watered with a mixture of milk and distilled water, using twelve parts of water to one of milk. Then another circle was drawn and the mandrake dug up, by which time the carving marks should have disappeared and the mandrake have grown to resemble a person. It should then be heat dried in the smoke of vervain leaves or else leaves of lemon verbena. The drying process could take up to three months after which the mandrake was ready for use as a hearth *magistellus* or guardian familiar.

An older tradition has it that the mandrake or mandragora root should be torn up at the foot of a gibbet, and by using a dog tied to the root because it was likely that the puller would die. With a mandrake a black witch could overthrow the reason of enemies, and change people into beasts, just as with the thorn apple she could cause men to dance till they died or make them submit to horrors of which they would later have no recollection.

In line with the story of mandrakes in Genesis, the plant was often used for its aphrodisiac properties, and also used in love charms were carrots, henbane, and myrtle. Of the mandrake it was also believed by some that the groan or scream given by the plant when extracted was tantamount to a death curse and that was one reason why a dog was used to pull it while the witch was out of earshot.

The 'black fast' referred to in Chapter 7 was a method used by black witches for inflicting a curse. The witch herself observed a fast for about two weeks after carrying out a full ritual of circle casting. During the fast no milk or milk product was taken and only water was drunk and a mere morsel of food eaten.

Another version of the 'black fast' was to fast strictly for nine successive Fridays along with a black hen. This would kill anyone who had stolen anything from the witch. During these fasts the witch concentrated all the power of her mind upon its purpose.

Personal curses given verbally were accompanied by a gesture given by aiming the left arm with the first two fingers extended, and sighting down them at the victim, closing the right eye and keeping the weight on the right foot. The 'black fast' would then follow if serious malice was intended.

In order to improve their powers of concentration some witches would resort to the bridle, a mask covering the entire head except the mouth, for sensory deprivation. The witches' bridle was also sometimes used for some initiatory purposes to symbolize the blindness and bondage of the mundane world.

This bridle or witches' cradle as it was sometimes known, was a very confining and restricting contraption, cutting off normal senses of perception and used by only a few to gain the concentration needed for certain kinds of occult attainment. It was obviously dangerous to use and I have met various fakirs in India who have acquired aspects of extrasensory perception through self-torture but who have lost the use of other faculties or of limbs in the process. There are simpler and more natural methods to gain powers of concentration.

Witchcraft can only operate if the practitioner draws upon his own reserves of power and unites them with that other reservoir of power which is universally present, and the same might be said of any religion, or any truly artistic pursuit. The casting of spells is really the use of a knowledge of natural law, and of the forces we all possess. Only those who are illuminated mentally know what Mind is but it cannot be explained any more than electricity really can, or radiation, or magnetism, or other invisible forces.

Curses and blessings have been unquestionably believed in for many centuries. During the new era of 'scientific' rationalization it has been said that only ignorant, superstitious people could possibly credit such ideas. More lately however, through discoveries in parapsychology, it has been admitted that a concentration of thought-force along with a powerful emotion such as love or hate can transmit and transfer a good or bad influence.

The oldest principle of magic is that of mimicry. When a doll of wax or other material is made it is usually given the name of the enemy it represents. By sticking pins in it or by other means of torture the belief is that the victim will suffer agonies in reality. It is an imitation of the hoped-for event.

Sceptics who scoff at such ideas may recall occasions of some stress such as being driven too fast in a car, and pressing their foot down on an imaginary brake. In the logical mind it is known that this will not affect the over-fast driving, but underneath is the old principle of imitation. To imitate what the driver should be doing is to try and make him do it.

Regarding bewitchment by puppets, dolls, poppets, mommets, mummets, or whatever other name might be given them, they were usually made of clay or wax, though other materials can be used. A very complicated ritual preparation was performed and baneful herbs ground up and mixed into the material along with whatever might be obtained from the intended victim, such as hair, nail parings or pieces of clothing. The best size for a mommet is between five and eight inches in length, and the correct sex should be depicted as well as extremities such as hands and feet. After being ritually anointed, needles, pins, nails, or thorns were used on the image or dagyde.

Curses were removed from herds of cows by taking a cow's heart and sticking it full of pins before roasting it in an oven. If a pig died through witchcraft its heart was stuck with pins and white thorns and hung in the chimney to prevent the rest of the pigs from being overlooked.

The evil power of a witch could also be withstood by the burning of sulphur, which had great properties for purification. The gall of a black dog put into perfume was another means, or the blood of the dog could be smeared on the walls of the infested house. Other protections were the carrying of a bible or a prayer book, or a piece of mistletoe or a four-leafed clover, or a piece of rowan wood which had grown out of another tree, or a bit of cinquefoil. Jasper could be worn against apparitions, while coral worn by infants gave them protection, and *antirrhinum* worn on a bracelet prevented poisoning.

The witch bottle was much employed in anti-spell practices by cunning men. Such bottles were often of a special shape and secret ingredients were securely sealed into them, then the bottle was heated. The black witch would then suffer agonies, as if his or her blood was boiling. When the miscreant arrived to beg for mercy, this was only granted if the original curse was withdrawn. Sometimes it was the operator's own nail parings which were placed in the stone jar to be placed on the fire or in the oven. Alternatively the hair, nail clippings, and urine of the bewitched person could be placed in the witch bottle. Or the urine poured on to a red-hot horseshoe sometimes had the same combating effect.

Witch hazel, elder, and holy water were all used as anti-witchcraft charms. Another method for defeating bewitchment was to take three small-necked stone jars and to place in each one the liver of a frog stuck full of new pins and the heart of a toad stuck full of thorns from a churchyard thornbush. The jars were then sealed and buried by three different churchyard paths, 7 inches from the surface and 7 inches from the church porch. While doing this the Lord's Prayer was repeated backwards. Then as the hearts and livers decayed, so did the maleficent power.

Genuine curative properties are contained in urine for external application, and it was much used in the village of my childhood for the eradication of chilblains. Before applying red lead to the metal of his ship the knowledgeable boatswain mixes urine with it for the best results in preventing rust. It was also used for curing skins and furs and fulling cloth, because it removed excess lanoline, and it also provided saltpetre.

Such simple practical knowledge is that of the genuine witch and urine with its antiseptic properties was often an integral part of several of her cures. I have also seen the application of fresh hot cow dung to the chest of an ailing child, and remarkable cures result from this old method of the wise woman. It has recently been conceded that such matter contains healing enzymes.

Many of the old remedies have been derided as ridiculous yet many have been found to be based on sound medical knowledge. Penicillin mould and digitalis are two of the better known instances.

A murderous witches' spell was that of obtaining some urine of the enemy, and then to buy a hen's egg without haggling over the price. Then on a Tuesday or a Saturday night the egg was taken into a field. A hole was made in its broad end and the white poured out, leaving the yolk. The egg was then filled with the urine while calling out the name of the enemy, and was then sealed with a piece of wet unused parchment. Next the egg was buried and the operator returned home without once looking back. As the egg decayed, the victim was attacked by jaundice. There was no cure unless the egg was withdrawn by the one who had buried it. If this was not done the victim died within a year.

More kindly in intent was a cure for ague in which an apple was cut into three parts on which were written 'Deus Pater', 'Deus Filius', and 'Deus Sanctus Spiritus'. The patient then had to fast for three days. At midnight on the first day he must eat the section of the apple marked 'Deus Pater' and the next two on the successive midnights.

Green bay would keep away hellwains or wandering spirits of the poltergeist type.

To discover who had bewitched cows it was necessary to drive one of the animals into the field with some unclean garment on its back, on a feast day or holy day. Then the cow was beaten to drive it away, whereupon it would run to the door of the witch responsible and beat its head on the door, crying loudly. Or the intestines of a beast killed by witchcraft could be dragged home along the ground and hung over the fire. As they got hot and burned, so the witch was afflicted with burning pains. Or a charm could be repeated last thing at night, and a sheep's heart nailed to the front door, which was kept locked, and securely bolted and barred. The operator then had to sit up alone all night, and must on no account open any doors or windows until morning. To my knowledge this counter spell was performed by a farmer in recent years, and during the night he heard a violent knocking and a voice calling to be let in. When he opened the door at daylight, he found a neighbour lying dead on the step.

To draw blood from a witch was generally reckoned to break the spell she had cast. This had to be done by 'scoring above the breath', that is, by scratching her above the nose and mouth. Anne Hudson had her forehead scratched in 1650 by a man who then recovered his health. It was also done by proxy to Margaret Morton by Joan Booth on behalf of her son, who then got better. At Huddersfield in 1651 a Mrs Spivey drew blood from a witch called Hester France, and then regained her health.

To prevent horses from being hag-ridden by witches at night and left exhausted, the familiar horseshoe was nailed over the stable door or a 'hag' stone was hung on a wall of the cottage, this being a stone with a natural hole through it.

A post of rowan wood under a cross beam of the house prevented witches and spirits from entering. These witch posts as they are known can still be found in some old houses, and were often carved with crosses on them.

The death of a witch prowling at night could only be ensured by shooting her with a crooked sixpence or other piece of silver used as a bullet or musket ball.

In the Middle Ages jet was often called witches' amber, and ornaments of it were used against the evil eye and lightning. It was also ground into powder and burnt as a fumigant against plagues and fevers. Witches also employed jet for curing headaches, hysteria, epilepsy, and dropsy, as well as burning the powder in order to tell fortunes from the fumes. Sea witches and fishermen's wives would also scatter ground jet on cottage fires to ensure the safe return of the men.

The usual charm for home protection required an invocation to a hearth goddess such as Ops, Rhea, Hertha, Ceres, or Vesta, all equally interchangeable. Then the witch walked deosil around the house holding her ritual athame in her right hand and an egg in the other. When the proper rites had been performed the egg was buried under the threshold in a specially prepared box. Fields were often blessed in the same way to ensure crop fertility.

Other home insurances are such objects as horseshoes, old keys, glass floats, holystones, and certain herbs. These are hung over windows, on doors, and in hallways. Horseshoes should have been worn, the keys used, and the genuine witch-ball is a glass float which has been used in fishing, hollow, and made of green bottle glass. Holystones should be those formed by natural erosion. Such used objects need no occult charging. Herbs used for house protection are often a pot-pourri of cloves, lavender, orris root, and others of a similar kind. Some witches have a pentagram design somewhere in the house, which is the five-pointed star that has become the emblem of the 'magic' of show business and the 'stars' of the entertainment world. The witches' star pentagram has rather more to it in the way of inscribed runic symbols. There are witches who also value the small flint arrowheads which were the elf-bolts of our ancestors.

Amulets made in the shape of hollow glass walking sticks and filled with coloured sand or other materials were also hung up in houses as a protection against evil. These were popular as 'fairings' or gifts sold at village and market town fairs. I have one in my possession which was bought at Brigg Horse Fair in 1800. It was thought that night demons came in at north windows, and would be attracted by the coloured glass. They would attach themselves to it, too fascinated to move, and could be safely wiped away next daylight.

Those amulets worn on the person varied from bits of paper with charms written on them, to jewellery made of amber, jet, coral, and cornelian.

To prevent someone from carrying out a particular action a

binding of tanglefoot spell us used. For this it is necessary to obtain an object link from the intended victim, hair or clothing or something similar. The method is that of plaiting the hair into a red cord, or of tying knots in the clothing obtained, which obviously is best in a scarf or something of the kind. Like all maleficent spells it is carried out when the moon is waning.

The witches' ladder made of human hair with nine knots in it was another element in cord magic. White witches would cure ague by use of blessing cords and leathern thongs which were worn round the neck of the sufferer. Nine pieces of red wool were put round a child's neck to ward off scarlatina. Witch-woven cords were a common charm against the evil eye.

A woman who was being burnt as a witch at St Andrews in 1572 had a white collar made of many strings and knots. Much against her will it was taken from her. Her grief was understandable for she believed it would spare her the pain of the flames.

Some binding spells were made by the witch putting nine knots in a cord, tying one at each end and working inwards to an appropriate incantation. The cord was then buried with another spell. To reverse the spell the whole process had to be reversed.

Another spell required a cross of rowan wood tied in a special way with red string. Yet another form of the witches' ladder was a cord knotted at regular intervals with a feather from a black hen fixed into each knot. Another way to curse a victim was to knock three iron nails into the north side of a tree in the form of a triangle, naming the victim with each blow.

A footprint on turf or earth could be taken up and dried and used for magic, and as it withered and lost its shape, so did the body of the victim. If the footprint was left on the ground and pierced with nails or glass, then the victim could be lamed or killed by an accident to the foot. If sharp glass, quartz, charcoal, and bones were added to the footprint the victim would always have pain. Each spell had of course to be accompanied by the correct incantation.

The 'hand of glory' was an old magical item sold by black witches to burglars to prevent their discovery whilst inside premises they were rifling. It was the mummified hand of a hanged man, prepared by wrapping it tightly in a piece of shroud until all the blood was squeezed out of it. Then it was dried in an earthenware jar with salt and saltpetre and peppers for about two weeks. After this it was dried in the sun or else over a fire of fern and vervain. When ready for use candles were stuck between the fingers, and this grisly candlestick was supposed to cause occupants of a house to sleep through the burglary operation.

A different version of the 'hand of glory' was to prepare it in such a way that the fingers acted as candles. It kept a household asleep provided the occupants were already asleep when it was lighted. If the thumb would not burn, it meant that somebody in the house was still awake.

In the last decade of the eighteenth century a woman arrived at a hostelry called the Old Spital Inn, which was on a lonely moor. She asked to stay the night but said that as she had to leave very early she did not require a bed, but would sleep in a chair, and that if breakfast was prepared she could leave without disturbing others.

This arrangement was agreed to, but the landlord asked a maid to sleep in the room as well. After everyone had retired, the maid noticed a man's leg under the alleged woman's skirt. Pretending to be asleep, the girl then saw the man produce a dead hand and light it. He passed the hand before her face saying, "Let those who are asleep be asleep, and let those who are awake be awake".

Still feigning sleep the maid saw him set the hand on the table and go and open the door to call his accomplices. She leapt up and pushed him outside and locked the door, then rushed upstairs to wake the family. But she was unable to awaken anybody until she had been downstairs again and extinguished the hand, which she did by throwing a jug of milk over it. Then she was able to arouse the rest of the occupants of the inn. This story was reported to Charles Wastell in 1861 by Bella Parkin, who was the daughter of the maid.

Witches were charged with many things, devil worship, relations with infernal spirits, desecration of holy symbols, and with murder and general maleficence, including economic crimes of 'blasting the corn on the ground, fruits on the trees, herbs of the fields'.

There is little distinction between occult healing, prayer, or blessing, and destructive magic such as cursing, ill-wishing, and actual magical killing. The difference lies in the mind of the practitioner. The Christian disciples learned much of occult knowledge and although they healed people with this knowledge they ultimately killed Ananias and Sapphira.

The story, told in Acts, reveals the use of black magic. It must be always remembered that if the slightest thing goes wrong with this terrible double-edged weapon it rebounds back on to the head of its perpetrator.

Occult knowledge gives to its owner power to increase the volume of experience to the brain. Normally the brain only accepts the amount of knowledge it is capable of handling. This applies to the type of knowledge as well as its volume. If the adjustment made by the occultist is for creative purposes the result is white magic, if for destructive ends it is black. The reason why black magic rebounds and why its user must ultimately 'pay' for it, is simply because being destructive or damaging to the universal life force it is against Nature. Nature abhors a vacuum and will fill it by some means or other, attacking the force which is damaging it.

Forces of Nature were utilized or tapped by the old witches, and the countryside was the true home of the Craft which reflected the integral customs of British peasantry, old songs and strange legends and rural dancing. Those witches preserved as much as they could of the genuine medical lore of antiquity, and cured illnesses long before doctors were known. They were the practical psychologists and psychiatrists of their time, as well as being criminologists, tracking down lost property and discovering the guilty by cunning methods of interrogative investigation. They should not be simply dismissed as charlatans.

14

WITCHCRAFT TODAY

The word witchcraft is perhaps too loosely used today, particularly in some sections of the popular Press. People will often use the word to describe anything they are unable to understand or explain, such as Satanism and churchyard vandalism.

It is not often realized what single-mindedness is required to pursue an occult path. Many methods have been attempted to achieve positive consciousness, from simple wishful thinking to extremes of asceticism. The desire has led to extraordinary expressions of absurdity and feats of incredible stoicism.

Although supernormal release can be temporarily gained through sustained physical effort such as in mass frenzy, or dervish dancing, the real way is not that of deliberately induced hysteria, but rather that achieved by inner stillness, allowing the opening of the self to meaning. This is the means to the path of basic mystical experience as propounded by the high adepts of all established religions from Catholicism to Mohammedanism, as well as by lesser mystical sects such as the Quakers, Subud, or Zenshu. It also correlates with the basic artistic experience.

It can be a dangerous area in which the mystic seeks deep religious expression, where witches and other psychics activate physical manifestations, and where the artist searches for creative expression. Forces are invoked which surpass anything that the ordinary consciousness can achieve. When such matters cannot be understood the mundane, easiest reaction is to dismiss them as either fraud or delusion.

Certainly many accused of witchcraft in the past have been hysterical, deluded, or insane. Others have cherished the intentions, but lacked the powers.

There are people who are born with psychic ability. Sometimes those so gifted are unaware of it. When the ability is manifested these people are called mediums, clairvoyants, telepaths, mystics, faith healers, geniuses, depending on the way the ability is utilized.

The gifted enter into a rapport with some aspect of Nature through which they can express their own inner being, which is of the same order of life force. A smaller universe is created which reflects the larger. Anyone can be briefly touched by a realization of unknown depths in Nature through some natural phenomenon such as a lovely sunset or other scene of grandeur, beauty, or tranquillity.

Witches believe in a pagan religion concerned with the mysteries, and they have a belief in reincarnation in a way that is somewhat similar to the expression of Hindu doctrine. Their faith is pantheistic, in which the god permeates all things. As a mystery religion, admittance to the Craft is by initiation and as previously point out, there is no central overall organization.

Sharing a conviction that anyone in need of the old religion will naturally gravitate towards it, witches do not try to convert others to their beliefs, and I know of no genuine coven that actively seeks new members. They are intelligent enough to know that anyone temperamentally unsuitable would derive no benefit and might only damage the existing circle. Consequently only certain selected people are allowed to pursue an inclination towards the Craft.

True modern witch covens operate independently and usually consist of six couples, male and female, in addition to a high priest or priestess. Many covens prefer thirteen members because witchcraft is a moon cult and there are thirteen moons to the yearly cycle, and some prefer to have a high priestess because of the ancient principle of a fertilizing goddess.

As already stated it is not always easy to join a real coven and membership has to be approved by all, and only when he has graduated from the third degree of the cult to the first will the newcomer be permitted to take part in all of the rituals. The duality and unity of Nature is expressed by the alternation of male and female members. In my own opinion several covens suffer from a social composition of middle-class intellectuals and humbler folk in an attempted fusion of authentic surviving folk tradition with the more intellectual middle-class occultism.

A Lincoln imp-symbol of
the medieval carver.

The insignia of the witch coven is generally a triangle over the five-pointed star. With both together, the pentangle has eight points and thirteen sides, thus symbolizing the eight ritual and thirteen lunar months.

Sabbats are celebrated at midnight of the night before the festival day. In the year are eight sabbats, and thirteen new-moon esbats and thirteen full-moon esbats. The sabbats are Yule on 21st December, counting as the beginning of the religious year with the winter solstice, and it might come as a surprise to learn that the word 'jolly' is derived from Yule. Next comes Candlemas, a fire festival on 2nd February, this once being the occasion on which new members were initiated.

Then comes the spring rite of 21st March, a celebration for fertility of men, crops, and animals. After that comes Roodmas, 1st May and Walpurgis Night, another fertility sabbat. Beltane is the festival for celebrating midsummer and the summer solstice on 21st June.

This is followed by Lammas on 1st August which marked the end of the wheat harvest and on which rites were performed for the increase of material supply. The autumn equinox rite was held on 21st September when thanksgiving was made for the blessings of the year. To complete the cycle is Hallowmas or Hallowe'en on 31st October when reunion of souls takes place, and divination made by the use of nuts, and spiritualist-type messages are received. These were the original sabbats, though some alleged covens have made their own modifications.

The activities of witchcraft are divination, healing, evocation, exorcism, spiritual or occult development, and the psychic charging of objects such as talismans. Working is done with the four elements of earth, air, fire, and water, and also on the astral plane. Healing is done by sympathetic magic, direction of will, and by herbalism. The herbalism differs somewhat from the ordinary kind because occult properties of the plants are also considered. Where used to prevent the actions of someone, binding spells can cause the person to have an accident or illness. There may also arise the necessity of countering such spells.

The original old religion had no knowledge of cabbalistic magic and though some so-called covens have adopted from that lore within the last hundred years or so, these influences are really foreign to the witchcraft tradition. Certainly witchcraft practice has evolved and gained accretions, particularly in the field of divination, but the cabbalistic tradition is in a different occult stream coming under the heading of sorcery, which is not the subject of this book.

In the formation of a coven it is important from the outset to decide its nature, and purpose. If fertility rites are a major symbolism, then the coven should have a high priest and a high priestess.

Covens stressing knowledge and power aspects have a male leader known as the magister, his female counterpart being the lady or queen. Second to these is a man called the officer, executor, or summoner. He traditionally wore black as a designation of his rank and for that reason found his way into the old trial records as 'the man in black'. His other badge of office is a blackthorn staff, which gave rise to another title of black rod, a title still used in Parliament as the Gentleman Usher of the Black Rod. The coven summoner is the secretary and first lieutenant, and can deputize in the absence of the magister, and in French covens he is often dressed in green and has the title of verdelet.

The lady sits on the right hand of the magister at meetings, and usually acts as a mediumistic seer under the control of the magister, when required. She also leads several ceremonies and most of the dances.

Most initiations are given from one sex to the opposite sex, though in non-goddess covens this rule is not rigidly applied, and it need not apply from parents to children.

Contrary to popular belief, nakedness is not a condition of attendance, nor is it necessary. The argument has been put forward that nudity prevents any restriction of the physical and psychic energies given off during certain rituals. This argument is fallacious because it would be a meagre kind of power that was hampered by clothing of any kind. It sometimes seems to me more of an argument for titillation or worse, than a genuine theory.

Certainly most modern meetings are held in warm rooms in these less hardy days and perhaps frenzied dancing building up to an intoxicating release of energy might require a state of nudity for some people, though this is by no means a tradition, but rather an idea pleasing to sensationalists in popular media.

Today the circle which is the sanctuary from dangerous forces is prepared in advance. Where possible it is an eleven-foot radius marked out by tape, chalk, or rope. Outside in the open air it would be cut in the earth by the athame.

Inside the circle is an altar upon which receptacles for water, salt, and ritual biscuits are laid. There are also some candles and sometimes a statuette of the goddess. Also inside the circle is a wine chalice known as a quaitch, a wand, an athame, a sword, and incense burners, and sometimes the Book of Shadows, with a few other ritual instruments as may be required.

The underlying idea of many of the rituals is to generate psychic power from the assembly and direct its force. A desired end may be that of healing a sick person, or it may be some material requirement. Some of the higher initiates can act as a store for this energy and render it usable. There are also rituals designed to produce occult knowledge of the continuance of existence through harmony with Nature.

The evocation of what are known as 'cones' of power is a way of using and directing psychic energy. This directing is what might be called the casting of charms or spells.

Each individual witch possesses an athame, either made by its owner or inherited. It is a black-handled knife properly charged and having runic symbols carved on its hilt. Another variety of the ritual knife is the bolline, differing only from the athame in having a curved blade. In my possession is a bolline which was bequeathed to me by a Yemeni witch.

When the first circle of a meeting is traced, ideally by the point of the knife or the sword, it is purified by use of water and incense. The altar candles are lit and others placed outside the circle. A prayer is made to the goddess and then members join the high priestess within the circle.

Initiation of a new member should be done during a sabbat. The novice is hoodwinked and led to the circle by the summoner to be duly initiated by the magister if female or by the lady if male, or by other first-degree witches in their absence. In some covens the members wear robes, and the magister should be wearing his horned headgear. The circle has been ritually prepared previously and the male and female aspects of power invoked, and the initiation ceremony is to release the applicant from mundane ties, his purification being by the four elements. He must not have any metal objects on his person. When the summoner has led the applicant to the north of the circle, the selected challenger touches the newcomer on the chest with an athame and asks from whence he came.

The tyro replies that he comes from the north, the place of darkness, to which is rejoined the question of whence does he go.

Having received the reply, to the east to seek the light, the challenger asks for the password of perfect love and perfect trust. Then the challenger tells the candidate that he cannot be admitted until purification has taken place and asks who will vouch for the newcomer.

As guider of souls, the summoner vouches for the applicant, who is then told by the challenger to enter from the darkness and receive the blessings of earth. Next the candidate's hands are bound loosely behind his back with the witches' cingulum, a ritual cord or girdle, with one end taken around his neck and down over the chest. His ankles are then fastened by a red cord, loosely enough to enable him to walk, and consecrated salt is sprinkled over him and a kind of medallion with the pentacle of earth inscribed on it is put between his lips.

The summoner leads him in the deosil direction around the perimeter of the circle, to stop at the west. After the earth symbol has been removed from his lips, the novice is again challenged as before but is given the blessing of water, taking a sip from the quaitch, and drops are sprinkled on his forehead. Led round the circle again, the candidate then ends up at the south to be challenged yet again, and blessed by fire, burning incense being swung before his face. A final circuit is made to the east, symbolic of air and light. Here, after the last challenge, the challenger breathes three times on the forehead of the candidate and then removes the blindfold to bestow light. The dramatic solemnity of this is sometimes enhanced by ensuring that the first thing seen is the magister, wearing his blazing, candle-topped and horned head-dress.

Purified by the four elements, the candidate is brought into the circle at north and his hands and feet untied. The magister or the lady then extends the athame towards the kneeling candidate who repeats a ceremonial oath of loyalty and secrecy, using his witch name and keeping his right hand on the blade of the knife.

In most covens the novice then adds his signature to those in the Book of Shadows. The witch name is personally selected and will remain secret within the coven. Some choose names of legendary witches, while others prefer a name reminiscent of their own astrological birth sign. Ideally the name should be reflective as an appropriate verbal symbol of the individual's personality.

Many covens take the measure of the newcomer by using a cord to gauge his height. The cord is kept, and the height recorded in the Book. Often a drop of blood and a few hairs are also taken to ensure fidelity from the new member. Reprisal can be taken by the coven through possession of these link objects if the newcomer proves to be treacherous.

Actually the correct way of taking the measure is by using white cotton to measure around the head, then tying a knot at the end of the measurement. The chest is then measured from that knot and another knot added, then the cotton is taken round the hips and knotted again. Next the measure from head to feet is taken, after which the cotton should be wound round the forefinger which is pricked so that a drop of blood is incorporated in the measure, which is then broken off at the last knot.

In some initiation ceremonies the ritual is concluded by the magister or lady placing a hand on the head of the kneeling candidate and calling down blessings on the new initiate and formally declaring his acceptance into the Craft.

Sometimes the new member is presented with the instruments of the coven to show that henceforth he shares in their use. These are objects such as the Book, pendants, the sword, chalices, censers, jewels, and so on. The coven then continues with its other business, and festivities with cake, wine, and dancing.

The athame has already been described and it is the main working implement of the witch for drawing circles and for other purposes such as cutting a divination wand, which should be from a hazel tree, and of a length measured from elbow to the tip of the middle finger. Wherever possible such objects should be ritually purified whilst still in the raw-material stage, but articles that are bought can still be purified providing that the golden rule is observed that their price is not bargained.

The quaitch or chalice is made of horn or of metal, being used for ritual purifications, for drinking from, and sometimes for mixing potions in. Censers are usually of the standard thurible type, or may be some other kind of burning dish.

All purification of objects is done by using a form of words over fire represented by incense or over salt cast into water, representing earth and water.

Circles cast for coven use should be of an 11-foot diameter, but a circle for solo use only should be of a 9-foot diameter. They should be marked out in a deosil direction, beginning and ending at the east.

The cingulum or girdle cord is red, having certain knots in it, and it can be used to make measurements for a circle.

Garters are worn above the left knee, and are made of leather, velvet, silk, or snake skin, or a combination of these things, and fastened by a silver buckle. They are only worn publicly at coven meetings. The relationship to the Order of the Garter has been described in a previous chapter.

Other personal witch adornments are copper or silver bracelets inscribed with the grade symbol of the wearer, a pentacle for second degree, and a triangle for the first degree. Necklaces worn by female witches should be of multiples of nine or thirteen beads. The beads are of various choice, including wood, metal, stone, acorns, amber, jet, or turquoise among other selections. Rings are also of personal choice.

After initiation the next step for the novice is the development of will power and concentration. There are several methods for learning how to concentrate, from gazing at an object, to the repetition of formulas, and the way to witchcraft is the way of years of patient observation.

The difference between genuine psychic vision and pathological hallucination is one that the true visionary has no need to argue, for real vision is on a level of consciousness beyond imagination or hallucinogenic effects.

When at last concentration is being mastered, the tyro must learn something about incantations and traditional charms. Besides these standards, simple rhyming couplets are devised on occasion, bearing in mind that the target for these rhythms is the practitioner's own subconscious, and therefore the formulas need to be potent enough to stir the deep recesses of the mind.

People of gregarious temperament usually find they achieve their best results by being involved in group repetition.

It is of no use for an untrained enthusiast to attempt anything for which they lack the faith, knowledge, and will power, for this is only to try something which their mind tells them is impossible. It has to be realized that the unconscious mind is just as important as the conscious mind, but that it is deeper, more vast in its potential extent, and lying in the cosmic field and therefore holds metaphysical powers. Incantations and rituals are only as important as they are allowed to be. Conviction of their validity is what ultimately makes them effective. Mere crude rhythm without any real melody is devoid of intellectual meaning and is powerful as a means of causing hysteria induced by the hypnosis of frenzy. This finds a corresponding chord in the immature mind, a phenomena which can be observed among many 'pop' fans.

There are of course gentler methods to induce the true way of discovery, which is that of converting intellectual understanding into deep insight. The mother instinctively knows the gentler method when she croons to her baby. Animals are also easily soothed and hypnotized by such means.

For rituals of divination and conjuration a pentagram or a hexagram should be worn for protection. Conjuration is dangerous and can rebound. Such pentacles should be about four or five inches long to take all the symbols to be inscribed on them. They are generally drawn on Saturdays at midnight and charged by the athame, then sewn into a bag of red silk, or of leather, to be hung around the neck.

As will have been seen, practices of witchcraft vary in different covens. Some covens are serious in intent and are composed of genuine witch membership, like two on the south bank of the River Humber, not far from my home. Such covens do not necessarily have thirteen members, nor do they meet with rigid regularity. More often than not they are small gatherings of initiates meeting to discuss matters of mutual interest, for the exchange of advice, for a little ordinary social fellowship, and for renewal of friendship. Ritual is at a minimum and initiation at meetings is rare because most of these people are country witches who pass their lore on to selected members of their own families, and who are individual practitioners of the Craft. Occasionally there is a hand-fasting ceremony, a witches' wedding that unites a couple not merely until death, but beyond into future lives. Such people as these country witches still survive within the communities of the world, but in most cases the urban populations are unaware of their existence.

The powers to be tapped are there in the mind, in oneself, in Nature. Focusing by group action is necessary to most people perhaps, but it is a relative concept, and the solitary witch, providing the knowledge and control of the will is present will achieve results in a quieter way.

The banding together in the way that some self-professed witches do today is modern urban concept, untypical of the old tradition of the Craft.

Some are carried away by the vanity of a paraphernalia of items for worship, and by fancy hierarchies and titles, hugging a delicious sense of secrecy to themselves which may allow them a pathetic feeling of superiority over workmates in office or factory.

Many genuine witches prefer to work more or less alone, with occasional meetings for consultation and conference or a sabbat.

The traditional forenames given to girls in witch families are of course also given unwittingly in non-witch families, but even today there are no traditional witches who do not name their daughters from the following kinds of names: Alice, Annie, Anna,

Anne, Hannah, Christine, Christianne, Eliza, Elizabeth, Betty, Bella, Lubella, Ellen, Helen, Isobel, Isobella, Janet, Jane, Joan, Joanna, Meg, Maggie, Peg Marian, Mary, May, and Maria.

There are of course others, and a lesser number for boys, but a full list would become a tedious recital.

It is only proper in a book on the subject of witchcraft to warn against those sects which practise black magic. Some of these masquerade under claims that they are for the study of astrology, or psychic development in one form or another. People have gone to such ostensibly innocent groups in good faith and prompted by the best of motives, only to find that they have been drawn into associations with sinister purposes.

It is time to leave when the first indications arise of an insidious undermining of individual moral standards begins. Many a weak-minded or unstable person has become enmeshed in diabolical practices from which he has been unable to escape without expert help. By then it has often been too late and all that has been left is a future of increasing degradation, insanity, and death. It should be remembered that evil intentions are linked with evil forces. Curious thrill seekers should try and be sensible enough to avoid the temptations of forbidden practices, because however light-hearted the initial approach may be, the ultimate penalty is always the same, and there is literally the Devil to pay.

This might also be the place to mention the abuse of drugs. To give the mind over to such an abuse is to render that mind defenceless. It is allowing the conscious personality to be taken over by the immobilizing forces of the subliminal consciousness. The visions which ensue, whether they be ecstatic or horrible are uncontrolled by any rationale, and the defences of the complete mind are temporarily destroyed. Habitual abuse quickly leads to a diminishing of real knowledge and mental order. Natural mental insulation goes the way of inhibition, and therein lies the danger.

The basis of our ancient folk belief is sadly neglected because of the contempt which materialistic industrialization produces, the traditional culture of the working population has been greatly eroded in this era of conditioning to artificial values. Yet survivals of our old heritage cling on tenaciously here and there.

When mankind has gone full circle in exhausting his stock of mechanical dependence, and the means of supporting it he will have to choose between a robot existence or a way of life in keeping with natural laws of intelligence. Indeed the necessity for such a choice is already with us.

There are feelings within us that seem indefinably, yet surely, to concern some mysterious order beyond this life, but which we also feel affect our lives, yet these feelings have been allowed to become complicated and rarely to find conscious expression. Many people think that if they tried to express such feelings in terms of a belief in some supernatural design they would sound ridiculous, or even a little insane. For the feelings involve a 'primitive' method of thinking which the modern civilized man has, or is reputed to have, discarded.

The true witches have accepted and expressed these feelings for so long now that they do not see anything unusual or uncivilized about a regard for the multiplicity of signs and portents and circumstances that hurtle around our destinies or lurk observing, about our lives.

And now that conservation and anti-pollution measures are of world concern, we can see that our animistic ancestors showed good intelligence in many of their beliefs. When every tree, stream and field was supposed to have its own protective deity, there was an attitude of careful husbandry which cannot be despised. The spirit of Nature was recognized and ceremonially assured that only the minimum of fruit would be gathered, trees felled, game caught, and grain harvested. The witches knew that Nature wronged and despised would revenge herself.

SELECT BIBLIOGRAPHY

Ahmed, Rollo, *The Black Art* (1936)

Boulton, R., *Compleat History of Magick, Sorcery and Witchcraft* (1725)

Franklyn, Julian, *Death by Enchantment* (1971)

Gould, Rupert T., *Oddities*

Hartmann, Franz, *Magic White and Black* (1938)

Kramer, Heinrich and Sprenger, James, *Malleus Maleficarum*, *trans*. M. Summers (1928)

Murray, Dr. Margaret, *The Witch Cult in Europe* (1921)

Rudkin, Ethel H., *Lincolnshire Folklore* (1936)

Scott, Sir Walter, *Letters on Demonology and Witchcraft*, reprinted 1884,

Shah, Idries, *Oriental Magic* (1956)

Summers, Montague, *Witchcraft and Black Magic* (1946)

Woodhouse, S. C., *Classical Mythology*

The Strange and Wonderful History of Mother Shipton (1686)

INDEX